This book can teach you basic Spanish in the simplest and fastest way. You will learn it here as you would in Mexico City, Caracas, or Madrid, by picking it up gradually from everyday events and by thinking of them in Spanish. This volume in the LOOK AND LEARN SERIES shows you essential Spanish in the most direct and dramatic way—by pictures which give you a look-and-learn view of the language uniting the more than 200,000,000 citizens of the Spanish-speaking world.

Every volume in the new LOOK AND LEARN SERIES is written by a prominent teacher especially for these editions. Professor Francisco Ibarra, now Director of The Academy of Languages, New York City, is also author of *Spanish Self-Taught*, and co-author of *French Self-Taught* and *Modern Russian Self-Taught* (Random House).

Laurel Look And Learn Series

LOOK AND LEARN FRENCH
by Anna Balakian,
Associate Professor of French Education, New York University.

LOOK AND LEARN RUSSIAN
by Aron Pressman,
in Charge of The Department of Russian, Washington Square College of Arts and Sciences, New York University.

Look And Learn SPANISH

FRANCISCO IBARRA

Director and Professor of The Academy of Languages, New York City

Illustrated by Aliki Brandenberg

A LAUREL EDITION

Published by DELL PUBLISHING CO., INC.
750 Third Avenue, New York 17, N. Y.

DEDICATION: To C.A.S. and W.D.C.

Typographic design by R. Scudellari

First printing—March, 1962

Printed in U.S.A.

Contents

Author's Note

The aim of *Look and Learn Spanish* is to introduce the reader to the Spanish language as it is spoken and heard, written and read. The emphasis of the book is on the spoken language, which is presented in a graded series of practical, everyday situations. These situations are presented with such simplicity of image and text that early recourse to either the vocabulary or the grammar is practically unnecessary. The result is early and sustained attention to the sounds and stresses proper to the language.

The ability to pronounce Spanish properly is the key not only to being understood but also to understanding in the language of the Spanish-speaking world. Accordingly, your attention is directed first of all to pronunciation—to the Spanish alphabet and to the sounds it represents—then to the syllables of spoken Spanish words, with their static stresses and with their fluid stresses in phrases and sentences. You will find that you will acquire a faster, surer command of sound and stress if you take this pronunciation section seriously, pronouncing every word, phrase and sentence carefully, clearly, repeatedly, and aloud. Then when you reach the pictorial section, which is the heart of the book and of the method, you will know how to use the syllabic stresses shown there in boldface type (sim**pá**tico).

The scheme of the pictorial section provides that you learn the vocabulary by means of pictures. A glance at each picture will give you the clues necessary not only to its caption, but also to the situation each picture helps to develop. The situations are related to each other and add up to the story of a family and their friends. At the end of each situation you will find a series of questions and answers. These are given to acquaint you with the Spanish word-order of both questions and answers.

Consult the vocabulary only if you are unable to derive the word from picture and situation. The vocabulary will give you the English equivalent of the word and, in special cases, refer you to rules in the grammar section which govern the uses and forms of the word. The verbs in the vocabulary are all keyed to the verb charts in the grammar section, which give the conjugations of the verbs.

To return to the use of the pictorial section, study each situation thoroughly. Do not shift suddenly to a new situation because you consider the one in hand too simple; go over it until you know it well. Expand it. Change *Yo soy norteamericano, inglés,* to *Yo soy venezolano, chileno,* etc. (I am an American, an Englishman; I am a Venezuelan, a Chilean.) Fill in the outlined map. Then say—out loud—*La Argentina está en Sud America. La Argentina es un país grande, no es pequeño. Buenos Aires está en la Argentina. Buenos Aires es la capital de la Argentina. El señor Martín es argentino. El señor Martín es argentino, pero él está ahora en los Estados Unidos,* etc. (Argentina is in South America. Argentina is a large country, not a small one. Buenos Aires is in Argentina. Buenos Aires is the capital of Argentina. Mr. Martín is an Argentine. Mr. Martin is an Argentine, but he is now in the United States.) This sort of exercise will teach you the difference between *ser* and *estar* (to be), and the Spanish names of the countries, capitals, and nationalities of our neighbors.

Every situation appears in the present tense. After you have learned the present, you should rework the picture section using the other tenses as they are introduced. This is work, but it is not busy-work; it is the way to learn Spanish.

Pronunciation Guide

The Spanish Alphabet

The following are the letters of the Spanish alphabet together with their usual names in Spanish.

A	a	*a*	J	j	*jota*	R	r	*ere*
B	b	*be*	K	k	*ka*		rr	*erre*
C	c	*ce*	L	l	*ele*	S	s	*ese*
Ch	ch	*che*	Ll	ll	*elle*	T	t	*te*
D	d	*de*	M	m	*eme*	U	u	*u*
E	e	*e*	N	n	*ene*	V	v	*ve*
F	f	*efe*	Ñ	ñ	*eñe*	W	w	*doble ve*
G	g	*ge*	O	o	*o*	X	x	*equis*
H	h	*hache*	P	p	*pe*	Y	y	*ye, i griega*
I	i	*i*	Q	q	*cu*	Z	z	*zeta, zeda*

You will note that *ch, ll,* and *ñ* are listed as single letters. In dictionaries and vocabularies, they are listed after *c, l* and *n* respectively. The names of the characters are feminine: *la a, la be, la ce, la che,* etc.

The Spanish Sounds

Fundamentally, Spanish vowels have but one sound. There are slight variations but these are automatically determined by the consonant that follows or precedes the vowel.

Spanish consonants are seldom as strongly pronounced as English consonants; but they must be pronounced distinctly for they control the vowel-sounds.

Spanish articulation is much more definite and clear-cut than English. Spanish is essentially a language of vowels; whereas English is more nearly a language of consonants. The gliding sound of so many English vowels—for example, of the "o" in "no"—is seldom heard in Spanish. Unstressed as well as stressed vowels are pronounced clearly, not slurred as in English. In learning to pronounce Spanish, try to use Spanish sounds, not English sounds. Don't think too much about the consonants, think about the vowels.

The stress of the Spanish words in this section is shown by boldface type. Use it, pronouncing each word aloud several times as you go.

THE VOWELS

a as English *a* in *father:*
casa, para, cara, carta

e as English *e* in *rest:*
este, tres, enero, ese

i as English *i* in *machine:*
sí, mil, insistir

o as English *o* in *obey:*
solo, por, poco, como

u as English *u* in *rule:*
lunes, útil, uno, nunca

THE CONSONANTS

b *and* **v** are pronounced exactly alike in Spanish. At the beginning of a sentence, or breath group, and after the letter *m* or *n*, they are pronounced as the English *b* in *book*, but less strongly:

boca, vamos, hombre, invitar

In all other cases they are pronounced as the English *v*, but are formed with both lips instead of upper teeth and lower lip; let the breath come lightly through the lips:

abril, libro, sábado, primavera

c before *a, o, u,* or a consonant, as English *c* in *cat:*

casa, como, Cuba, clase

Before *e* or *i* this letter is pronounced as English *th* in *think;* but as English *s* in *see* in Southern Spain and the Americas:

centavo, once, cinco, cerca

ch as English *ch* in *cheer:*

muchacho, Chile, leche

d at the beginning of a sentence, or breath group, and after the letter *l* or *n*, as English *d,* but with the tip of the tongue against the upper teeth:

dos, domingo, donde, día

otherwise, as English *th* in *father:*

madre, padre, adiós, cuidado

f as English *f* in *father:*
falta, flor

g before *e* or *i,* as Spanish *j,* below:
gente, página

at the beginning of a sentence, or breath group, and followed by *a, o, u* or any consonant, and after the letter *n,* as English *g* in *go:*
gustar, gracias, domingo

otherwise, much more softly:
alegre, agua, amigo

gue *and* **gui** as English *gue* and *gui* in *guest* and *guitar* (note that the *u* is silent):
guerra, guisante, seguir, Guillermo

güe *and* **güi** as English *gue* and *gui* in *unguent* and *extinguish* (note that *ü* is sounded):
vergüenza

h is always silent:
hasta, hombre, hablar

j as English *h* in *house,* but with more rasp:
mujer, José, lejos, hijo

k as English *k.*

l as English *l* in *like,* but with the tip of the tongue against the gums of the upper teeth:
libro, lejos

ll as English *ll* in *million,* except that the Spanish *ll* has a single and uniform sound (mi-llón) and not the double sound of the English *ll* + *i* in *million* (mil-lion); but as English *y* in *yes* in Southern Spain and the Americas:

calle, ella, Guillermo, ellos

m as English *m:*

martes, mes

n as English *n,* but softer:

nada, anoche

When followed by *c* or *g,* this letter has a sound similar to the English *ng* in *sing:*

cinco, lengua

ñ as English *ny* in *canyon:*

año, España, español, niño

p as English *p* in *spot,* but more softly, and without the puff of breath:

pero, para, papel, poco

que *and* **qui** as English *ke* and *ki* in *keg* and *kiss* (*q* is found only before *e* and *i;* note that the intervening *u* is silent):

quince, porque, quizás, quedar

r has a strong rolling sound at the beginning of a word and when it comes after *l, n,* or *s:*

radio, responder, rico, Enrique, Israel

In all other cases it is very slightly rolled:

pero, caro, sobre, primero

rr The strong rolling sound of *r* between two vowels is always expressed by *rr* (this is treated as a single letter, like *ch* and *ll*):

perro, arriba, carretera, guerra

s as English *s* in *see:*

sábado, casa

t as English *t* but more softly, with the tip of the tongue touching the upper teeth rather than the gums:

tarde, tres, también, tener

v See ***b*** above.

w as English *w,* or as in the foreign word where it appears.

x between vowels, as English *x* (*ks*), or as English *gs:*

exacto, éxito

before consonants, as English *x* (*ks*), or as Spanish *s:*

explicar, extraño

in some words of Mexican origin, as Spanish *j:*

México, mexicano

y as English *y* in *yes,* but stronger:

yo, ya, ayer

alone, as English *i* in *machine:*

y

at the end of a word, it is short and weak:
hoy, muy

z as English *th* in *think;* but as English *s* in *see* in Southern Spain and the Americas:
zapato, marzo, azúcar, brazo

THE DIPHTHONGS

In speaking or writing Spanish, one must take care never to divide a diphthong. The vowels of the diphthong should be so pronounced that they fuse into one utterance.

The diphthongs are combinations consisting either of a strong vowel and a weak vowel, or of two weak vowels. The strong vowels are *a, e* and *o;* the weak vowels are *i, u,* and final *y.*

In the mixed diphthongs, the stress falls on the strong vowel:

causa, pausa, seis, siete, bien, cuatro, nuevo, bueno

In the weak diphthongs, slight stress falls on the latter of the two weak vowels:

ciudad, cuidado, muy

Syllables

A word has as many syllables as it has vowel sounds or vowel combinations.

A single consonant between two vowels forms a syllable with the following vowel:

ga-so-li-na, mu-cha-cho, ma-ña-na, e-lla, a-rri-ba

Note that the letters *ch, ll,* and *rr,* being treated as single letters, also form a syllable with the following vowel.

Two consonants between vowels are usually separated so that one belongs with the preceding and the other with the following vowel:

cer-ca, in-sis-tir, en-ten-der, im-por-tan-te

The two consonants are not separated when the second is *l* or *r,* except *lr, rl, sl, tl.* For example:

pa-dre, ha-blar, li-bro, a-bril, blan-co

but:

al-re-de-dor, is-la

Prefixes form separate syllables when one writes:

des-a-gra-da-ble

but not when one speaks:

de-sa-gra-da-ble

Stress and Written Accent

Words ending in a vowel, a diphthong, or in the consonants *n* or *s,* are stressed on the next to the last syllable:

ca-sa, ca-sas, bue-no, bue-nos, gra-cia, ha-bla, ha-blan, en-ten-de-mos

Words ending in a consonant (including *y*), except *n* and *s,* are stressed on the last syllable:

ha-blar, co-mer, vi-vir, us-ted, pa-pel

Words stressed contrary to the above rules bear the written accent over the vowel of the syllable to be stressed:

a-quí, in-glés, fá-cil, di-fí-cil, lá-piz, lá-pi-ces, lec-ción

A certain number of words bear the written accent in order to distinguish them from words like them in spelling and pronunciation but different from them in meaning:

él, el; dé, de; más, mas; sí, si; mí, mi; sólo, solo

The written accent is also used to distinguish the interrogative or exclamatory from the relative use of pronouns and adverbs, and demonstrative pronouns from demonstrative adjectives:

¿cuánto?, cuanto; ¿cuándo?, cuando; ¿cómo?, como; ¿qué?, que; ¿quién?, quien; ¿cuál?, cual; éste, este; éstos, estos

Linkage and Contraction

Spoken Spanish links words, with the result that two or more words may sound like one long word. These linked words are termed "breath groups," which are groups of words pronounced between pauses. A short sentence may be spoken as one breath group. A long sentence may be divided into several breath groups. A pause should never be made within the breath group because the breath group expresses a complete thought. Familiarity with linkage will enable you to understand spoken Spanish.

To link words within a breath group, carry the last consonant of a word over to the following word, when it begins with a vowel, a diphthong, or an *h* (the Spanish *h* is silent). This effect of the spoken language accords perfectly with the specification of syllables and stresses:

el hombre:	e-**lom**-bre
los hombres:	lo-**som**-bres
es el hombre:	e-se-**lom**-bre
por eso:	po-**re**-so
los Estados Unidos:	lo-ses-**ta**-do-su-**ni**-dos
el aire:	e-**lai**-re
los aires:	lo-**sai**-res
vamos a comer:	va-mo-sa-co-**mer**

While in written Spanish there are only two contractions, *del* and *al,* which are contractions of *de* + *el* and *a* + *el,* in the spoken language there are many. These contractions require special attention if we are to understand spoken Spanish:

¿Dónde están?: ¿**Dón**-des-**tán**?

Contraction does not occur when the following vowel is stressed:

es de él: es-de-**él**

Punctuation

Spanish punctuation is much the same as English, but inverted question and exclamation marks are used. The inverted mark is placed at the beginning of the actual question or exclamation, which is not always at the beginning of the sentence: *¿Cómo está usted? ¡Qué hermosa mujer! Usted es de Nueva York, ¿no es verdad?*

Los Estados Unidos

Yo soy norteamericano.
Soy norteamericano.

Yo soy norteamericana.
Soy norteamericana.

Nosotros somos norteamericanos.
Somos norteamericanos.

México

Usted es mexicano.

Usted es mexicana.

Ustedes son mexicanos.

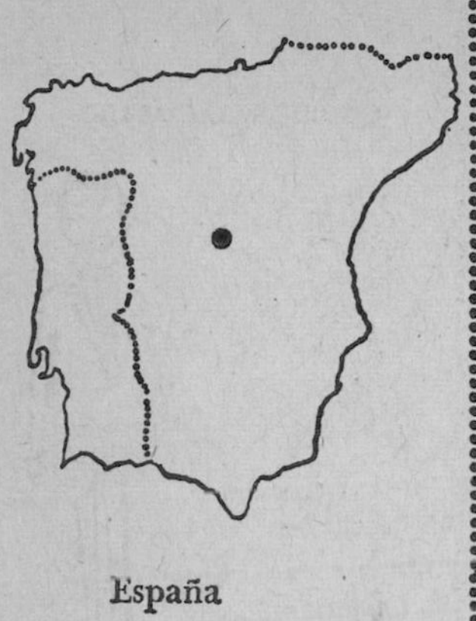

España

Él es español.
Es español.

Ella es española.
Es española.

Ellos son españoles.
Son españoles.

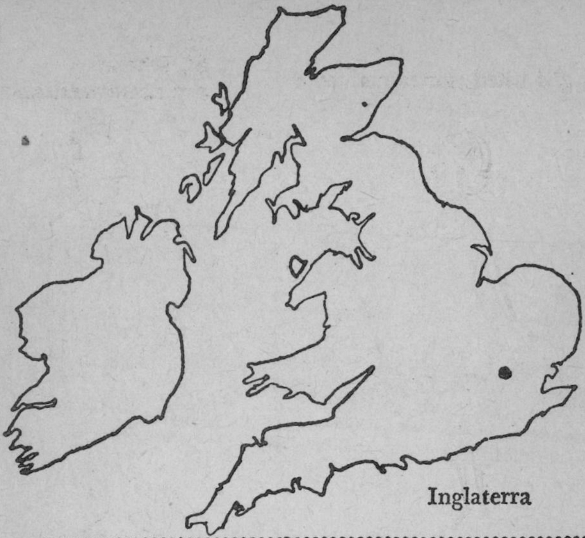

Inglaterra

Yo soy inglés
y ella es inglesa.

Nosotros somos ingleses.
Somos ingleses.

¿Es usted norteamericano?

Sí, señora;
soy norteamericano.

¿Es ella española?

No, es mexicana.

¿Son ustedes norteamericanos?

Sí, somos norteamericanos.

¿Son ellos ingleses?

No, él es español y ella es inglesa.

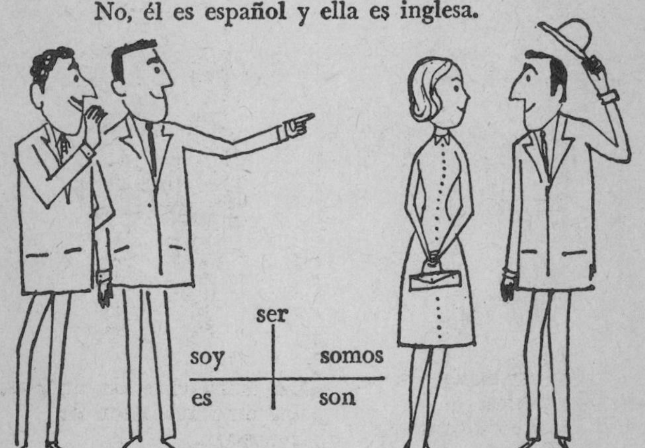

un hombre
el hombre

El hombre es norteamericano.
El hombre es de los Estados Unidos.

una mujer
la mujer

La mujer es mexicana.
La mujer es de México.

dos muchachos
los muchachos

Los muchachos son españoles.
Los muchachos son de España.

dos muchachas
las muchachas

Las muchachas son inglesas.
Las muchachas son de Inglaterra.

¿De dónde es el hombre?

El hombre es de los Estados Unidos.

¿De dónde es el hombre?
¿De dónde son los muchachos?
¿De dónde son las muchachas?
¿De dónde es usted?
¿De dónde soy yo?

Yo soy norteamericano.
Soy norteamericano.
Yo me llamo Francisco Adams.
Me llamo Francisco Adams.

El señor Adams.

Yo soy norteamericana.
Soy norteamericana.
Yo me llamo Elena de Adams.
Me llamo Elena de Adams.

La señora de Adams.

Usted es mexicana.
Usted se llama María Cruz.

Usted es mexicano.
Usted se llama José Juárez.

El señor Juárez.

La señorita Cruz.

Él es español. Es español.
Él se llama Miguel Cervantes.
Se llama Miguel Cervantes.

Ella es española. Es española.
Ella se llama Isabel de Cervantes.
Se llama Isabel de Cervantes.

La señora de Cervantes.

El señor Cervantes.

Ella es inglesa.
Es inglesa.
Ella se llama Carolina Winter.
Se llama Carolina Winter.

Él es inglés.
Es inglés.
Él se llama Guillermo Dalton.
Se llama Guillermo Dalton.

El señor Dalton.

La señorita Winter.

Nosotros nos llamamos Francisco Adams y José Juárez.
Nos llamamos Francisco Adams y José Juárez.

Ustedes se llaman Elena de Adams y María Cruz.

Ellos se llaman Miguel Cervantes y Guillermo Dalton. Se llaman Miguel Cervantes y Guillermo Dalton.

Ellas se llaman Isabel de Cervantes y Carolina Winter. Se llaman Isabel de Cervantes y Carolina Winter.

¿Cómo se llama usted?

Me llamo Francisco Adams.

¿Cómo se llama la señorita norteamericana?
¿Cómo se llama la señorita mexicana?
¿Cómo se llama la señorita inglesa?
¿Cómo se llama la señora española?
¿Cómo se llama usted?
¿Cómo nos llamamos nosotros?

llamarse

me llamo	nos llamamos
se llama	se llaman

Este hombre es norteamericano.

Ese hombre es inglés.

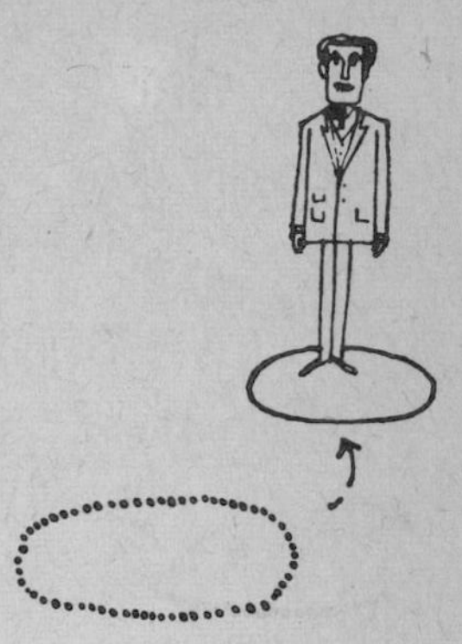

Aquel hombre es español.

Estos hombres son norteamericanos.

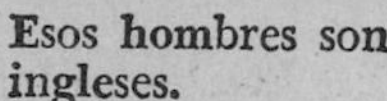
Esos hombres son ingleses.

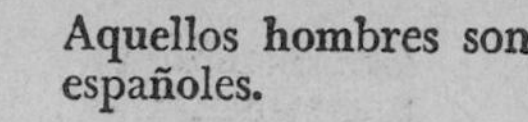
Aquellos hombres son españoles.

Esta mujer es norteamericana.

Esa mujer es inglesa.

Aquella mujer
es española.

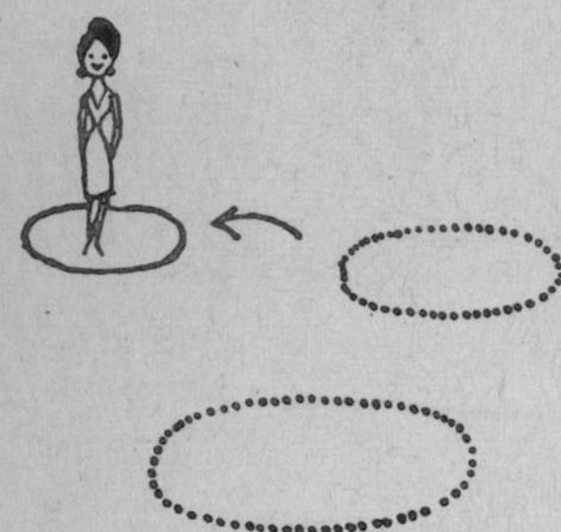

Estas mujeres son
norteamericanas.

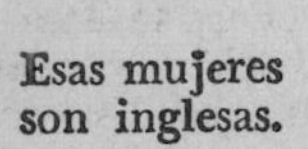

Esas mujeres
son inglesas.

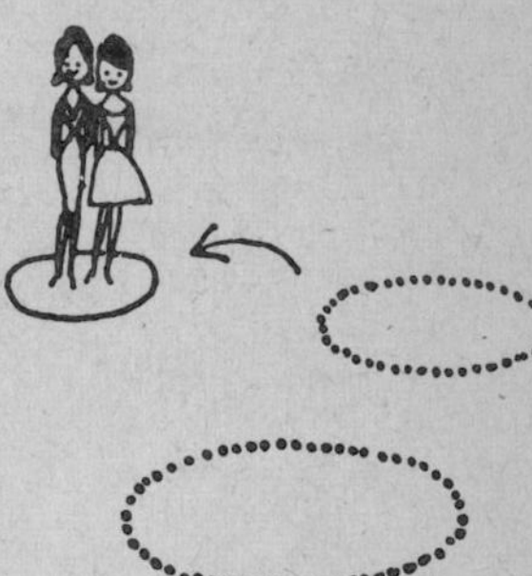

Aquellas mujeres
son españolas.

Este hombre y esa mujer son mexicanos.

Esta mujer y esos hombres son españoles.

Yo me llamo Francisco Adams.

Esta señora se llama Elena de Adams. Esta señora es mi mujer. Nosotros somos marido y mujer.

Yo me llamo Isabel de Cervantes.

Este señor se llama Miguel Cervantes.

Este señor es mi marido. Nosotros somos marido y mujer.

Este señor es su amigo. Su amigo de usted se llama José Juárez.

Esta señorita es su amiga. Su amiga de usted se llama María Cruz.

Miguel es nuestro amigo. Miguel es amigo nuestro.
Nuestro amigo se llama Miguel Cervantes.

Isabel es nuestra amiga.
Isabel es amiga de nosotros.
Nuestra amiga se llama Isabel de Cervantes.

Miguel e Isabel son nuestros amigos.
Ellos son amigos de nosotros.

Francisco y Elena son mis amigos.
Ellos son mis amigos.

José y María son amigos de Guillermo.
Ellos son sus amigos. Son amigos de él.

Esta señorita es amiga de los Cervantes,
del señor Dalton y de la señorita Cruz.
Ella es amiga de ellos.
Es su amiga.

¿De dónde es este señor?

Este señor es de Inglaterra.
Este señor es inglés.

¿Cómo se llama su amigo de usted?

Mi amigo se llama José Juárez.

¿De dónde es Guillermo?
¿De dónde es Carolina, la amiga de Guillermo?
¿De dónde es María?
¿De dónde es José, el amigo de María?
¿De dónde es este señor?
¿De dónde es ése?
¿De dónde es aquél?

¿Cómo se llama el amigo de la señorita Winter?
¿Cómo se llama la amiga del señor Juárez?
¿Cómo se llaman los amigos de los Adams?
¿Cómo se llaman estos muchachos?
¿Cómo se llaman ésos?
¿Cómo se llaman aquéllos?
¿Cómo se llama esta muchacha?

NÚMEROS

1 = uno (un), una
2 = dos
3 = tres
4 = cuatro
5 = cinco
6 = seis
7 = siete
8 = ocho
9 = nueve
10 = diez
11 = once
12 = doce
13 = trece
14 = catorce
15 = quince
16 = dieciséis
17 = diecisiete
18 = dieciocho
19 = diecinueve
20 = veinte
21 = veintiuno (veintiún), veintiuna
22 = veintidós
23 = veintitrés
24 = veinticuatro
25 = veinticinco
26 = veintiséis
27 = veintisiete
28 = veintiocho
29 = veintinueve
30 = treinta
31 = treinta y uno (un), una
32 = treinta y dos
33 = treinta y tres
40 = cuarenta
41 = cuarenta y uno (un), una
42 = cuarenta y dos
43 = cuarenta y tres
50 = cincuenta
51 = cincuenta y uno (un), una
60 = sesenta
70 = setenta
80 = ochenta
90 = noventa
100 = ciento (cien)
101 = ciento uno (un), una
102 = ciento dos

116 = ciento dieciséis
150 = ciento cincuenta
200 = doscientos, -as
201 = doscientos uno
300 = trescientos, -as
400 = cuatrocientos, -as
500 = quinientos, -as
600 = seiscientos, -as
700 = setecientos, -as
800 = ochocientos, -as
900 = novecientos, -as
1,000 = mil
1,300 = mil trescientos, -as
2,000 = dos mil
15,000 = quince mil
100,000 = cien mil
500,000 = quinientos, -as mil
1,000,000 = un millón
2,000,000 = dos millones
1960 = mil novecientos sesenta

Yo tengo treinta y un años.
Yo soy mayor que mi mujer.

Mi mujer tiene veintinueve años.
Mi mujer es menor que yo.

Nosotros tenemos dos hijos: un hijo y una hija.
Nuestro hijo se llama Juanito.
Nuestra hija se llama Anita.
Juanito tiene ocho años. Anita tiene seis años.
Juanito es mayor que su hermana Anita.
Anita es menor que su hermano Juanito.

Nuestro amigo Miguel tiene veinticinco años.
Su mujer tiene veinticinco años también.
Ellos tienen la misma edad.

Guillermo tiene cuarenta años.
Carolina tiene treinta y ocho.
Ellos son mayores que nosotros.
Nosotros somos menores que ellos.

tener	
tengo	tenemos
tiene	tienen

Francisco Adams tiene padre y madre. Los padres de Francisco Adams son los abuelos de sus hijos Juanito y Anita. Ellos son nietos de los padres de Francisco Adams.

Francisco Adams tiene dos hermanos: un hermano y una hermana. Sus hermanos son tíos de sus hijos Juanito y Anita. Ellos son sobrinos de los hermanos de Francisco Adams.

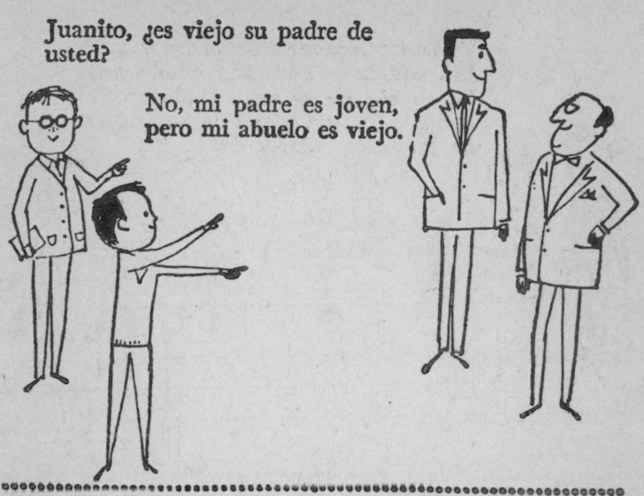

Juanito, ¿es viejo su padre de usted?
No, mi padre es joven, pero mi abuelo es viejo.

Juanito, ¿es vieja su madre de usted?

No, mi madre es joven, pero mi abuela es vieja.

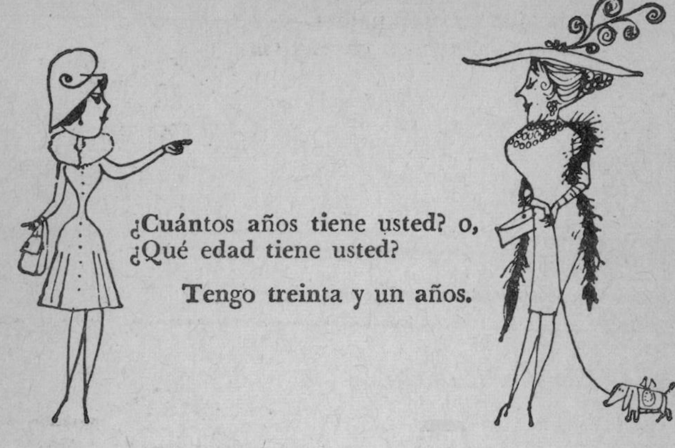

¿Cuántos años tiene usted? o,
¿Qué edad tiene usted?
Tengo treinta y un años.

¿Cuántos años tiene usted?
¿Cuántos años tiene su esposa?
¿Quién es mayor, usted o su esposa?
¿Cuántos años tiene Isabel?
¿Cuántos años tiene el esposo de Isabel?
¿Quién es mayor, Isabel o su esposo?
¿Cuántos años tiene Guillermo?
¿Quiénes son mayores, ellos o nosotros?
¿Cuántos años tiene la hermana de Juanito?
¿Quién es menor, Anita o su hermano?
¿Tiene usted padres?
¿Son viejos sus padres?
¿Tiene usted tíos?
¿Son jóvenes sus tíos de usted?

Yo vivo con mis padres.
Nosotros vivimos en esta casa.

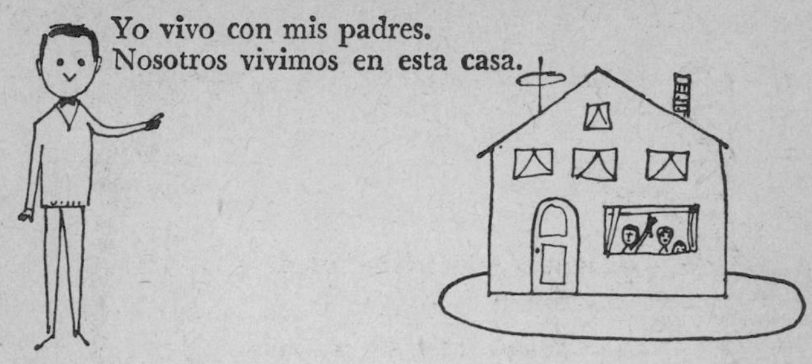

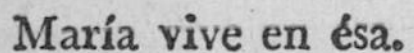

María vive en ésa.

Carolina vive en aquélla.

Guillermo vive en esta calle.

Los Cervantes viven en esa avenida.

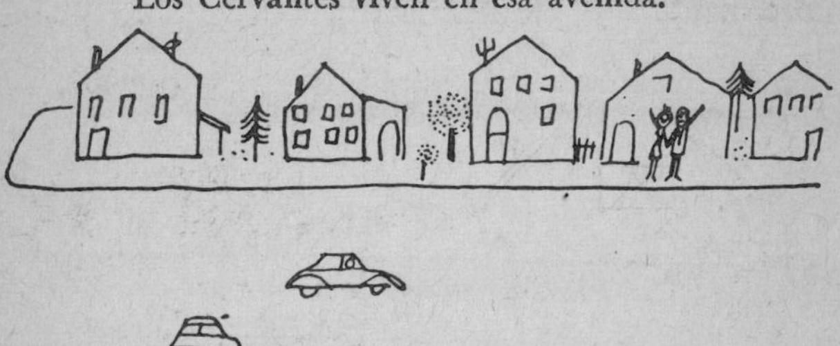

Nosotros vivimos en la avenida San Martín, número 15.

Mis amigos viven en
la calle 55, número 65, este.

María vive en la calle 52,
número 2, oeste.

José vive en la avenida
Mádison, número 3.

¿Con quién vive Juanito?

Juanito vive con sus padres.

¿Dónde viven ellos?

Viven en la avenida Mádison, número 15.

¿Dónde vive Carolina?
¿Dónde vive Guillermo?
¿Dónde viven los Cervantes?
¿Dónde viven los Adams?
¿Dónde viven los amigos de los Adams?
¿Dónde vive usted?
¿Con quién vive usted?

vivir

vivo	vivimos
vive	viven

Nuestra casa es grande y nueva.
Nuestra casa está en esta calle.

La casa de María es pequeña y blanca.
La casa de María está cerca de nuestra casa.

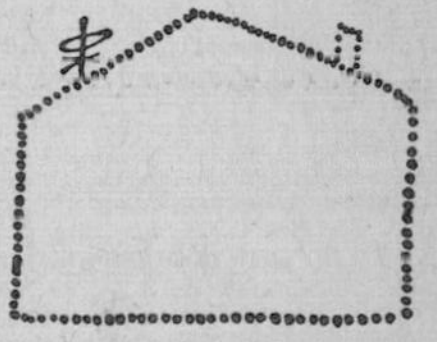

La casa de Carolina es vieja, pero muy bonita.
La casa de Carolina está lejos de nuestra casa.

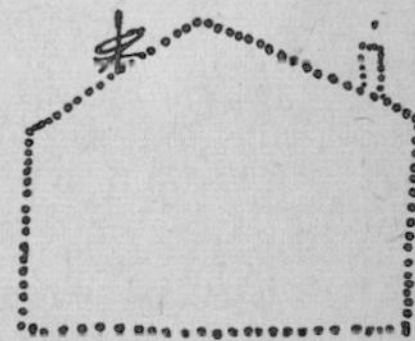

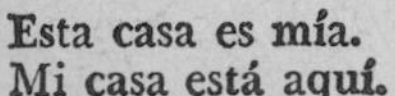

Esta casa es mía.
Mi casa está aquí.

Esa casa es de María.
La casa de María está ahí.

Aquella casa es de Carolina.
La casa de Carolina está allí.

Esta casa es mía, ésa es suya, aquélla es de Carolina.

Mi casa está aquí, la suya está ahí, la de Carolina está allí.

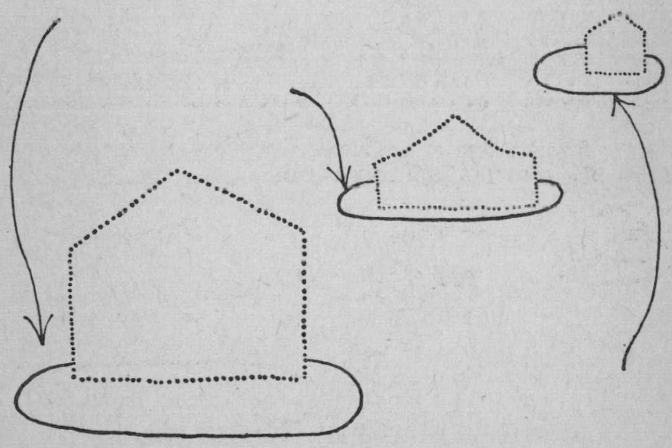

La casa de Guillermo
está en esta calle.

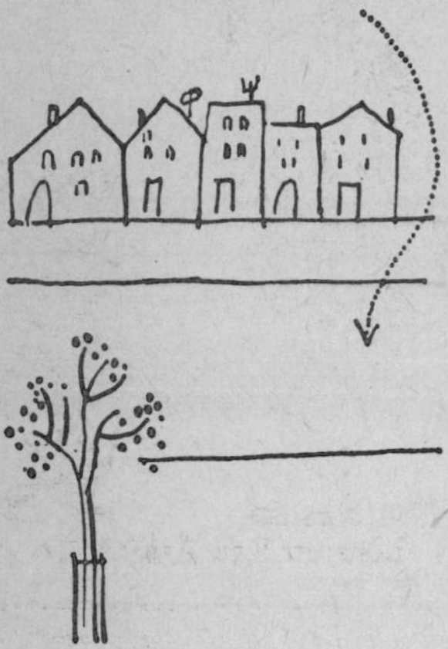

Guillermo no está ahora
en su casa, está en
su despacho.

La casa de los Cervantes
está en esa avenida.

Los Cervantes
están ahora
en Europa.

La casa de los Adams no está en el campo, está en la ciudad.

Ellos están ahora en Sud América.

La casa de los amigos de los Adams está en el campo.

Ellos no están ahora en el campo, están en la ciudad.

Yo soy profesor de español.
Yo no estoy ahora en mi casa,
estoy en la escuela.

Nosotros estamos en España, pero somos norteamericanos.

¿Cómo es nuestra casa?
¿Dónde está nuestra casa?
¿Cómo es la casa de María?
¿Dónde está la casa de María?
¿Dónde está la casa de Guillermo?
¿Dónde está Guillermo?
¿Dónde está la casa de los Cervantes?
¿Dónde están ahora los Cervantes?
¿Dónde está la casa de los Adams?

¿Dónde están ahora los Adams?
¿Dónde está la casa de los amigos de los Adams?
¿Dónde están ahora los amigos de los Adams?

estar

estoy	estamos
está	están

España es un país de Europa.
Inglaterra es otro país de Europa.

La Argentina es un país de Sud América.
Chile es otro país de Sud América.

Costa Rica es un país de Centro América.
Guatemala es otro país de Centro América.

México es un país de Norte América.
Los Estados Unidos es otro país de Norte América.

Sud América no es un país, es un continente.
Europa es otro continente.
Asia es otro continente.
África es otro continente.

El Perú es un país de Sud América.
El Perú está en Sud América.
Lima está en el Perú.
Lima es la capital del Perú.
Los peruanos viven en el Perú.
Los peruanos hablan español.

¿Qué es el Perú?
¿Dónde está el Perú?
¿Dónde está Lima?
¿Qué es Lima?
¿Dónde viven los peruanos?
¿Qué idioma hablan los peruanos?

¿Cómo se llaman los países de Sud América?
¿Cómo se llaman los países de Centro América?
¿Cómo se llaman los países de Norte América?
¿Cómo se llaman las capitales de los países de Sud América?
¿Cómo se llaman las capitales de los países de Centro América?
¿Cómo se llaman las capitales de los países de Norte América?
¿Qué idioma se habla en Colombia?
¿Qué idioma se habla en los Estados Unidos?

hablar

hablo	hablamos
habla	hablan

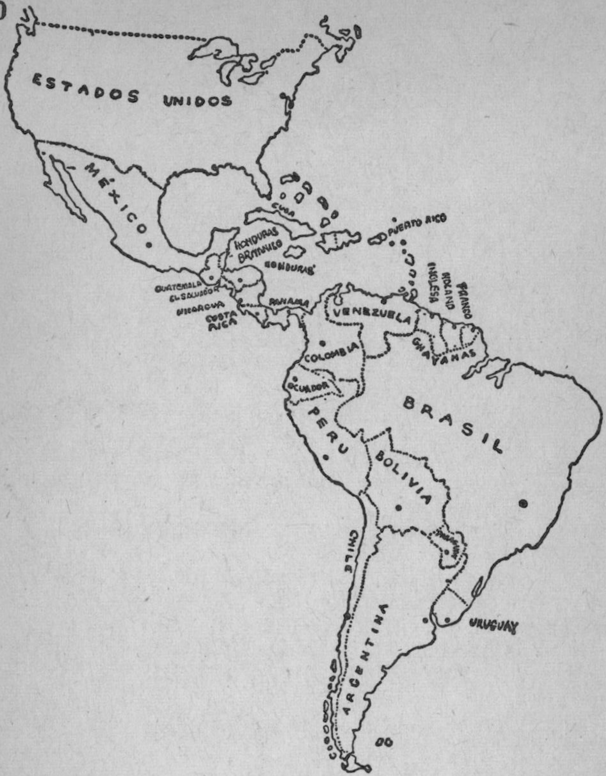

ESTADOS UNIDOS
MÉXICO
CUBA
PUERTO RICO
HONDURAS BRITANICO
HONDURAS
GUATEMALA
EL SALVADOR
NICARAGUA
COSTA RICA
PANAMA
VENEZUELA
INGLESA
HOLAND
FRANCO
GUAYANAS
COLOMBIA
ECUADOR
PERU
BRASIL
BOLIVIA
CHILE
ARGENTINA
URUGUAY

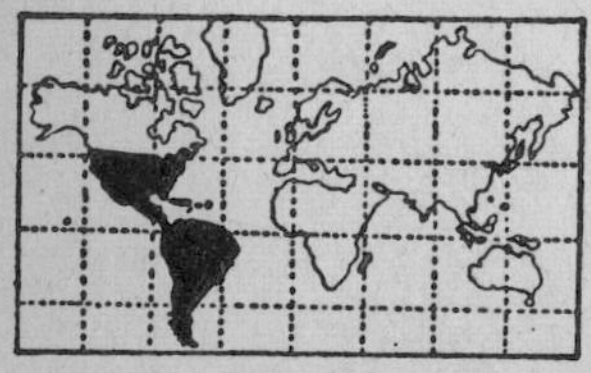

José es alto.
José es alto, pero es menos alto que Francisco.

Francisco es alto.
Francisco es más alto que José, pero es menos alto que Guillermo.

Guillermo es alto.
Guillermo es más alto que Francisco y José. Guillermo es el más alto de los tres.

Miguel es bajo

Antonio es bajo.
Antonio es más bajo
que Miguel.

Pedro es bajo.
Pedro es más bajo que Antonio
y Miguel. Pedro es el más bajo
de los tres.

María es alta.
María es alta, pero es menos alta que Elena.

Elena es alta.
Elena es más alta que María, pero es menos alta que Carolina.

Carolina es alta.
Carolina es más alta que Elena y María. Carolina es la más alta de las tres.

La casa de Francisco es grande, no es pequeña. La casa de Francisco es grande, pero es menos grande que la casa de Guillermo.

La casa de Guillermo es grande, no es pequeña. La casa de Guillermo es más grande que la casa de Francisco, pero es menos grande que la casa de José.

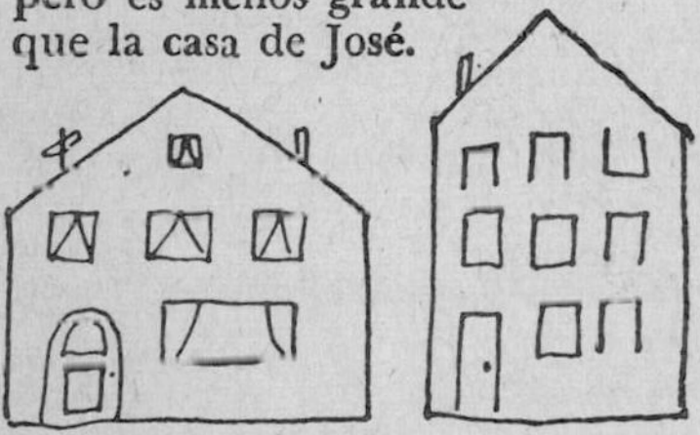

La casa de José es grande, no es pequeña. La casa de José es más grande que la casa de Guillermo y la casa de Francisco. La casa de José es la más grande de las tres.

La calle en que yo vivo es larga y ancha, no es corta y estrecha. La calle en que yo vivo es menos larga y ancha que la calle en que ellos viven.

La calle en que ellos viven es larga y ancha, no es corta y estrecha. La calle en que ellos viven es más larga y ancha que la calle en que yo vivo.

Este libro es bueno.

Ése es mejor que éste.

Aquél es el mejor
de los tres.

Estos libros son buenos.

Ésos son mejores
que éstos.

Aquéllos son los
mejores de todos.

Esta pluma es buena.

Ésa es mejor que ésta.

Aquélla es la mejor de las tres.

Estas plumas son buenas.

Ésas son mejores que éstas.

Aquéllas son las mejores de todas.

Este lápiz es malo.

Ése es peor que éste.

Aquél es el peor
de los tres.

Estos lápices son malos.

Ésos son peores
que éstos.

Aquéllos son los
peores de todos.

Esta luz es mala.

Ésa es peor que ésta.

Aquélla es la peor
de las tres.

Estas luces son malas.

Ésas son peores
que éstas.

Aquéllas son las peores
de todas.

¿Es José más alto que Francisco?
¿Cuál de los tres es el más alto?
¿Es Miguel más bajo que Antonio?
¿Cuál de los tres es el más bajo?
¿Es María más alta que Elena?
¿Cuál de las tres es la más alta?
¿Es pequeña la casa de Francisco?
¿Cuál de las tres casas es la más grande?

¿Es corta y estrecha la calle en que ustedes viven?
¿Cuál de las dos calles es más larga y ancha?
¿Es bueno este libro?
¿Cuál de los dos libros es mejor?
¿Cuál de los tres libros es el mejor?
¿Cuáles de todos estos libros son los mejores?

EL DÍA

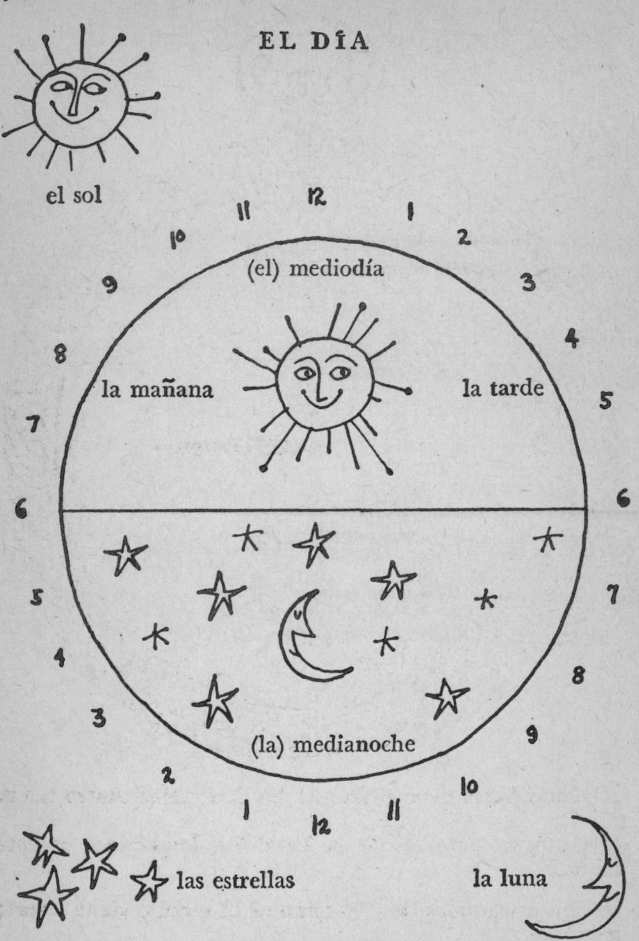

LA NOCHE

¿Cuántas horas tiene el día? El día tiene veinticuatro horas.

¿Cuántos minutos tiene la hora? La hora tiene sesenta minutos.

¿Cuántos segundos tiene el minuto? El minuto tiene sesenta segundos.

¿Cuántos minutos tiene la media hora? La media hora tiene treinta minutos.

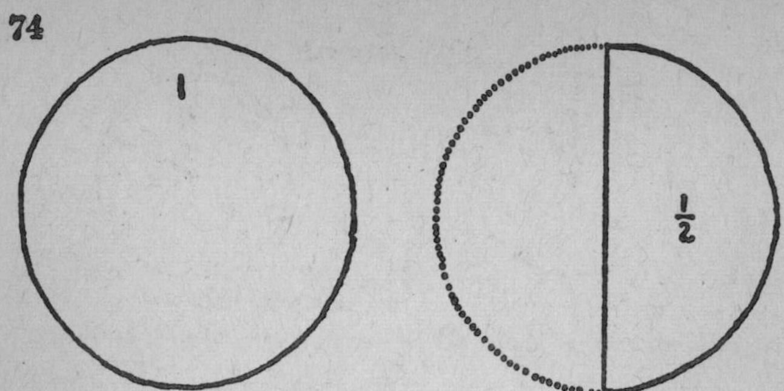

¿Cuántos minutos tiene la hora? La hora tiene sesenta minutos.

¿Cuántos minutos tiene la media hora? La media hora tiene treinta minutos.

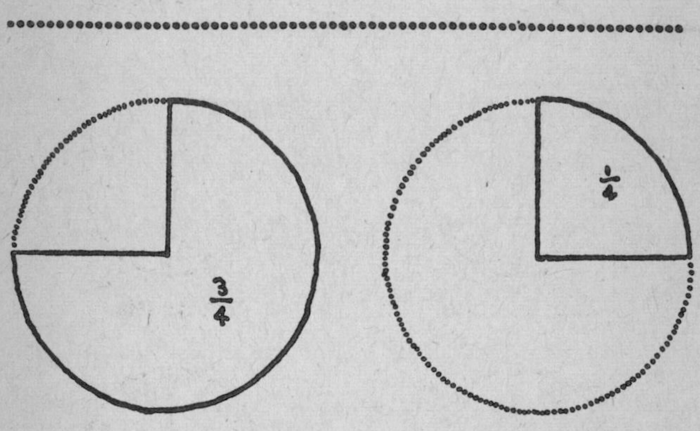

¿Cuántos minutos tienen los tres cuartos de hora? Los tres cuartos de hora tienen cuarenta y cinco minutos.

¿Cuántos minutos tiene el cuarto de hora? El cuarto de hora tiene quince minutos.

Es la una.
Es la una en punto.

Son las dos.
Son las dos en punto.

Son las tres.

Son las cuatro.

Son las cinco.

Son las seis.

Son las siete.

Son las ocho.

Son las nueve.

Son las diez.

Son las once.

Son las doce.

Es la una y cinco (minutos)

Son las dos menos veinte.

Es la una y diez.

Son las dos menos cuarto.

Es la una y cuarto.

Son las dos menos diez.

Es la una y veinte.

Son las dos menos cinco.

Es la una y media.

Son las dos.

Son las tres y veinticinco.

Son las cuatro menos diez.

Son las cinco menos cinco.

Son las cuatro menos cuarto.

¿Qué hora es, José?

Según mi reloj son las tres y media.

¿Anda bien su reloj?

No, se atrasa cinco minutos.

Entonces el mío se adelanta mucho.

¿Qué hora tiene el suyo?

El mío tiene las cuatro menos cuarto.

Yo voy a la escuela.

Voy a la escuela para estudiar y aprender el español. No hablo español, pero estudio mucho y aprendo un poco.

Él va a la escuela.

Va a la escuela para estudiar y aprender el español. No habla español, pero estudia mucho y aprende un poco.

Nosotros vamos a la escuela.

Vamos a la escuela para estudiar y aprender el español. No hablamos español, pero estudiamos mucho y aprendemos un poco.

El español no es difícil, es fácil.

Ellos van a la escuela.

Van a la escuela para estudiar y aprender el español. No hablan español, pero estudian mucho y aprenden un poco.

El español es una lengua muy importante.

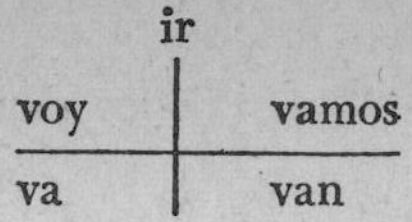

ir

voy	vamos
va	van

estudiar

estudio	estudiamos
estudia	estudian

aprender

aprendo	aprendemos
aprende	aprenden

Yo vengo a la escuela.

Vengo a la escuela para aprender a leer y escribir el español. En la escuela leo, escribo y hablo en español con el profesor. No hablo bien el español todavía.

Él viene a la escuela.

Viene a la escuela para aprender a leer y escribir el español. En la escuela lee, escribe y habla en español con el profesor. No habla bien el español todavía.

Nosotros venimos a la escuela.

Venimos a la escuela para aprender a leer y escribir el español. En la escuela leemos, escribimos y hablamos en español con el profesor. No hablamos bien el español todavía.

Ellos vienen a la escuela.

Vienen a la escuela para aprender a leer y escribir el español. En la escuela leen, escriben y hablan en español con el profesor. No hablan bien el español todavía.

venir

vengo	venimos
viene	vienen

leer

leo	leemos
lee	leen

escribir

escribo	escribimos
escribe	escriben

¿Qué hace usted en la escuela?

Hago muchas cosas. Es decir, hablo en español, leo en voz alta, y escribo las palabras y las frases.

¿Qué hace él en la escuela?

Hace lo mismo que yo.

¿Qué hacen ustedes en la escuela?

Hacemos muchas cosas. Es decir, hablamos, leemos y escribimos.

¿Qué hacen ellos en la escuela?

Hacen lo mismo que nosotros.

¿Qué dice el profesor del español?

Dice que el español es una lengua importante y que tengo que estudiar mucho.

¿Qué dice usted del español?

Digo lo mismo que mi profesor. Es decir, que el idioma español es muy importante.

¿Qué dicen ustedes del profesor de español?

Decimos que es muy buen profesor.

¿Dicen ellos lo mismo del profesor?

Ellos dicen que es excelente.

hacer

hago	hacemos
hace	hacen

decir

digo	decimos
dice	dicen

tener que + *infinitive*

tengo que	tenemos que
tiene que	tienen que

¿Qué hora es?
¿Adónde va usted?
¿A qué hora va usted a la escuela?
¿A qué viene usted a la escuela?
¿Habla usted español en la escuela?
¿Habla usted bien el español?
¿Lee usted el español?
¿Quién aprende un poco?

¿Qué hacemos nosotros en la escuela?
¿Qué hace él en la escuela?
¿Qué hace usted en la escuela?
¿Es difícil el español?
¿Es el español una lengua importante?
¿Qué lengua estudian ustedes mucho?
¿Qué lengua estudian ustedes en la clase?
¿Qué idioma se habla en este país?

Yo abro la puerta del cuarto.

Él abre la puerta del cuarto.

Nosotros abrimos la puerta del cuarto.

Ellos abren la puerta del cuarto.

Yo entro en el cuarto.

Él entra en el cuarto.

Nosotros entramos en el cuarto.

Ellos entran en el cuarto.

Abro la puerta y entro en el cuarto; luego cierro la puerta.

Abre la puerta y entra en el cuarto; luego cierra la puerta.

Abrimos la puerta y entramos en el cuarto; luego cerramos la puerta.

Abren la puerta y entran en el cuarto; luego cierran la puerta.

---

abrir

abro	abrimos
abre	abren

entrar

entro	entramos
entra	entran

cerrar

cierro	cerramos
cierra	cierran

Yo me quito el sombrero.

Él se quita el sombrero.

Nosotros nos quitamos el sombrero.

Ellos se quitan el sombrero.

Me quito el sombrero y voy a mi asiento.

Se quita el sombrero y va a su asiento.

Nos quitamos el sombrero y vamos a nuestros asientos.

Se quitan el sombrero y van a sus asientos.

Yo pongo mis libros sobre la mesa.

Él pone sus libros sobre la mesa.

Nosotros ponemos nuestros libros sobre la mesa.

Ellos ponen sus libros sobre la mesa.

Pongo los libros sobre la mesa
y me **siento al lado** de una **alumna.**

Pone los libros sobre la mesa y se
sienta detrás de una alumna.

Ponemos los libros sobre la mesa
y nos sentamos delante de un alumno.

Ponen los libros sobre la mesa y se sientan frente al profesor.

quitarse	
me quito	nos quitamos
se quita	se quitan

poner	
pongo	ponemos
pone	ponen

sentarse	
me siento	nos sentamos
se sienta	se sientan

¿Quién abre la puerta del cuarto?
¿Qué hacemos después de abrir la puerta?
¿Qué hacemos después de entrar en el cuarto?
¿Qué se quita usted cuando entra en el cuarto?
¿Qué nos quitamos nosotros?
¿Qué se quita la señorita?

¿Adónde va usted después de quitarse el sombrero?
¿Adónde vamos nosotros?
¿Dónde pone usted los libros?
¿Dónde ponen ellos los libros?
¿Dónde me siento yo?
¿Dónde se sienta él?
¿Dónde nos sentamos nosotros?
¿Dónde se sientan ellos?

Abro el libro y empiezo a estudiar mi lección

Abre el libro y empieza a estudiar su lección.

Abrimos los libros y empezamos a estudiar nuestras lecciones.

Abren los libros y empiezan a estudiar sus lecciones.

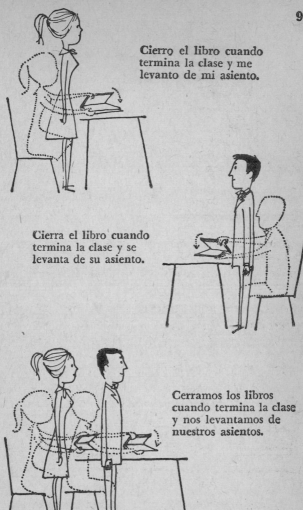

Cierro el libro cuando termina la clase y me levanto de mi asiento.

Cierra el libro cuando termina la clase y se levanta de su asiento.

Cerramos los libros cuando termina la clase y nos levantamos de nuestros asientos.

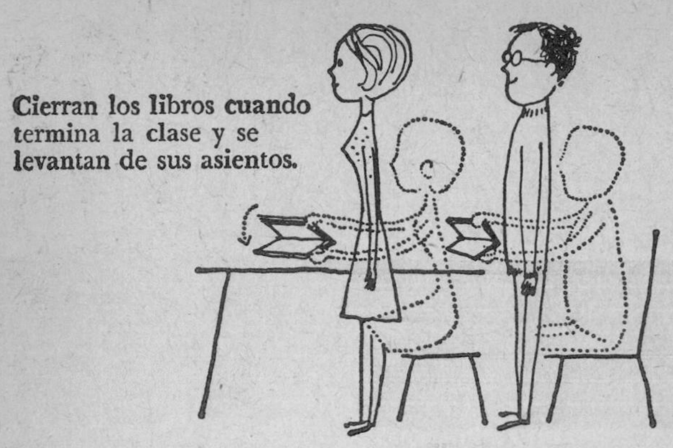

Cierran los libros cuando termina la clase y se levantan de sus asientos.

terminar	
termino	terminamos
termina	terminan

levantarse	
me levanto	nos levantamos
se levanta	se levantan

Tomo los libros y me despido del profesor y de mis compañeros de clase.

Toma los libros y se despide del profesor y de sus compañeros de clase.

Tomamos los libros y nos despedimos del profesor y de nuestros compañeros de clase.

Toman los libros y se despiden del profesor y de sus companeros de clase.

Me pongo el sombrero y salgo a la calle.

Se pone el sombrero y sale a la calle.

Nos ponemos el sombrero y salimos a la calle.

Se ponen el sombrero y salen a la calle.

tomar

tomo	tomamos
toma	toman

salir

salgo	salimos
sale	salen

despedirse

me despido	nos despedimos
se despide	se despiden

ponerse

me pongo	nos ponemos
se pone	se ponen

¿A qué hora empieza la clase?
¿Qué hacemos con los libros?
¿Qué hacemos cuando abrimos los libros?
¿Qué hace usted cuando abre el libro?
¿A qué hora termina la clase?
¿Qué hacemos cuando termina la clase?
¿Qué hacen ellos cuando termina la clase?

¿Qué toma usted antes de salir de la clase?
¿De quién se despide usted?
¿De quién nos despedimos nosotros?
¿Qué hago yo cuando me despido del profesor?
¿Qué se ponen ellos?
¿Qué se pone usted?
¿A dónde sale usted?
¿A dónde salen ellos?

Yo vuelvo a mi casa.

Después de la clase vuelvo a mi casa.
Llego a mi casa a las 4:30.

Él vuelve a su casa.

Después de la clase vuelve a su casa.
Llega a su casa a las 4:40.

Nosotras volvemos a nuestra casa.

Después de la clase volvemos a nuestra casa.
Llegamos a nuestra casa a las 4:45.

Ellos vuelven a su casa.

Después de la clase vuelven a su casa.
Llegan a su casa a las 5:15.

volver	
vuelvo	volvemos
vuelve	vuelven

llegar	
llego	llegamos
llega	llegan

Yo salgo de mi casa.

Salgo de mi casa temprano. Salgo a las 8:30. Salgo a las 8:30 de la mañana.

Él sale de su casa.

Sale de su casa tarde. Sale a las 3:15. Sale a las 3:15 de la tarde.

Nosotros salimos para Europa.

Salimos para Europa mañana por la mañana. Salimos por vapor.

Ellos salen para Sud América.

Salen para Sud América mañana por la noche.

Salen por avión.

El vapor sale a las 8:30 de la mañana (A.M.).

El avión sale a las 5:15 de la tarde (P.M.).

El tren sale a las 11:05 de la noche (P.M.).

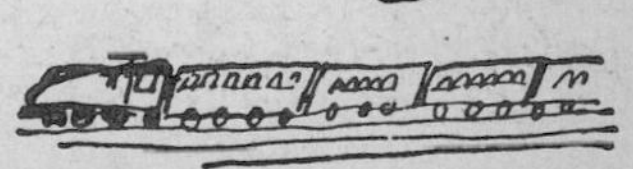

¿Quién vuelve a la casa?
¿A dónde vuelve usted después de la clase?
¿A qué hora llega usted a su casa?
¿A qué hora llegamos nosotros a nuestra casa?
¿A qué hora llegan ellos a su casa?

¿A qué hora sale usted de su casa?
¿Salen ellos para Europa?
¿Cuándo salimos para Europa?
¿Cuándo salen ellos para Sud América?
¿Salen ustedes de la casa tarde o temprano?
¿Salimos nosotros para Europa por la mañana o por la tarde?
¿Salen ellos por avión o por vapor?

LOS DÍAS DE LA SEMANA

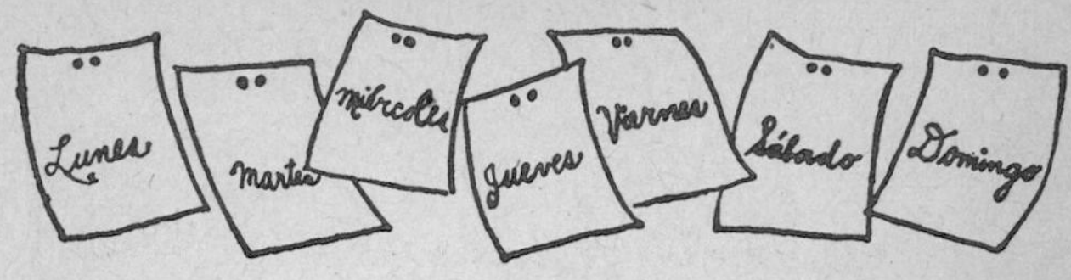

El lunes es un día de la semana.
Es el primer día de la semana.
Es el primero.

El martes es otro día de la semana.
Es el segundo día de la semana.
Es el segundo.

El miércoles es otro día de la semana.
Es el tercer día de la semana.
Es el tercero.

El jueves es otro día de la semana.
Es el cuarto día de la semana.
Es el cuarto.

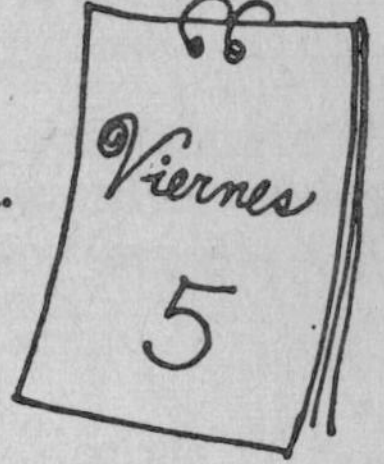

El viernes es otro día de la semana.
Es el quinto día de la semana.
Es el quinto.

El sábado es otro día de la semana.
Es el sexto día de la semana.
Es el sexto.

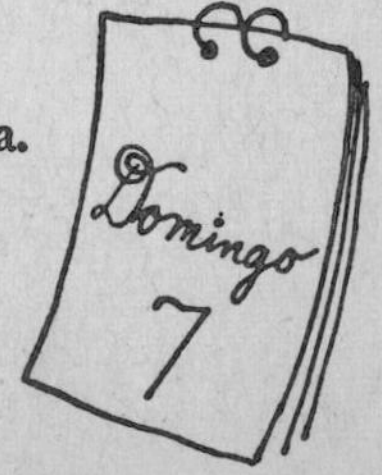

El domingo es otro día de la semana.
Es el séptimo día de la semana.
Es el séptimo.
Es el último día de la semana.

La semana tiene siete días.

Lunes	Martes	Miércoles	Jueves	Viernes	Sábado	Domingo
1	2	3	4	5	6	7
8	9					

Los días de la semana son lunes, martes, miércoles, jueves, viernes, sábado y domingo.

El lunes, el martes, el miércoles, el jueves y el viernes son días de trabajo.

Los lunes, los martes, los miércoles, los jueves y los viernes vamos a la

oficina, al campo,

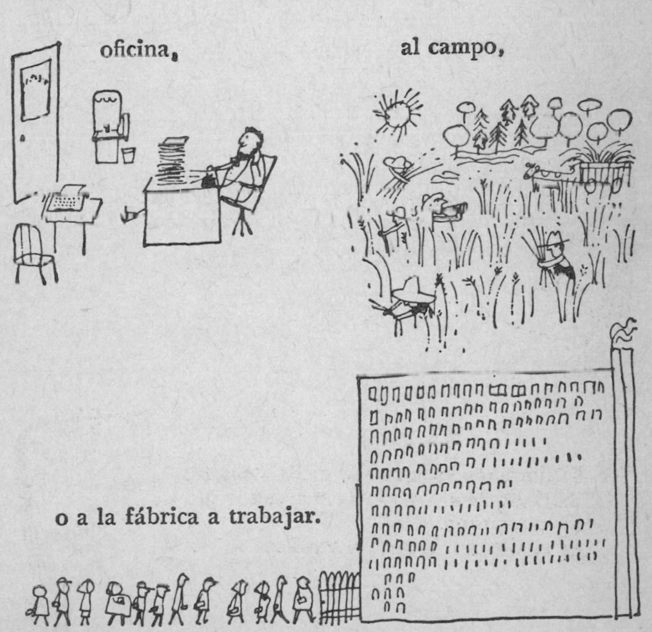

o a la fábrica a trabajar.

El sábado es día de diversión. Los sábados vamos al teatro,

al museo,

o al parque a pasear.

El domingo es día de descanso.

Los domingos vamos a la iglesia,

escuchamos la radio,

o miramos la televisión.

escuchar

escucho	escuchamos
escucha	escuchan

mirar

miro	miramos
mira	miran

trabajar

trabajo	trabajamos
trabaja	trabajan

pasear

paseo	paseamos
pasea	pasean

¿Qué es el domingo?
¿A dónde vamos los sábados?
¿Qué es el sábado?
¿A dónde vamos los domingos?
¿Qué día de la semana es hoy?
¿A dónde va usted mañana?
¿Qué día de la semana es mañana?

¿Cuántos días tiene las semana?
¿Cuáles son los días de la semana?
¿Qué son el lunes, el martes, el
miércoles, el jueves y el viernes?
¿A dónde vamos los lunes, los martes,
los miércoles, los jueves y los
viernes?

LOS MESES DEL AÑO

Enero es un mes del año.
Enero tiene treinta y un días.

ENERO						
1	2	3	4	5	6	7
8	9	10	11	12	13	14
15	16	17	18	19	20	21
22	23	24	25	26	27	28
29	30	31				

Febrero es otro mes del año.
Febrero tiene veintiocho o
veintinueve días.

FEBRERO						
1	2	3	4	5	6	7
8	9	10	11	12	13	14
15	16	17	18	19	20	21
22	23	24	25	26	27	28

Marzo es otro mes del año.
Marzo tiene treinta y un días.

MARZO						
1	2	3	4	5	6	7
8	9	10	11	12	13	14
15	16	17	18	19	20	21
22	23	24	25	26	27	28
29	30	31				

Abril es otro mes del año.
Abril tiene treinta días.

ABRIL						
1	2	3	4	5	6	7
8	9	10	11	12	13	14
15	16	17	18	19	20	21
22	23	24	25	26	27	28
29	30					

Mayo es otro mes del año.
Mayo tiene treinta y un días.

MAYO						
1	2	3	4	5	6	7
8	9	10	11	12	13	14
15	16	17	18	19	20	21
22	23	24	25	26	27	28
29	30	31				

Junio es otro mes del año.
Junio tiene treinta días.

JUNIO						
1	2	3	4	5	6	7
8	9	10	11	12	13	14
15	16	17	18	19	20	21
22	23	24	25	26	27	28
29	30					

Julio es otro mes del año.
Julio tiene treinta y un días.

JULIO						
1	2	3	4	5	6	7
8	9	10	11	12	13	14
15	16	17	18	19	20	21
22	23	24	25	26	27	28
29	30	31				

Agosto es otro mes del año.
Agosto tiene treinta y un días.

AGOSTO						
1	2	3	4	5	6	7
8	9	10	11	12	13	14
15	16	17	18	19	20	21
22	23	24	25	26	27	28
29	30	31				

Septiembre es otro mes del año.
Septiembre tiene treinta días.

SEPTIEMBRE						
1	2	3	4	5	6	7
8	9	10	11	12	13	14
15	16	17	18	19	20	21
22	23	24	25	26	27	28
29	30					

Octubre es otro mes del año.
Octubre tiene treinta y un días.

OCTUBRE						
1	2	3	4	5	6	7
8	9	10	11	12	13	14
15	16	17	18	19	20	21
22	23	24	25	26	27	28
29	30	31				

Noviembre es otro mes del año.
Noviembre tiene treinta días.

NOVIEMBRE						
1	2	3	4	5	6	7
8	9	10	11	12	13	14
15	16	17	18	19	20	21
22	23	24	25	26	27	28
29	30					

Diciembre es otro mes del año.
Diciembre tiene treinta y un días.

DICIEMBRE						
1	2	3	4	5	6	7
8	9	10	11	12	13	14
15	16	17	18	19	20	21
22	23	24	25	26	27	28
29	30	31				

El año tiene doce meses.

Los meses del año son enero, febrero, marzo, abril, mayo, junio, julio,

agosto, septiembre, octubre, noviembre y diciembre.

¿Cómo se llama el primer mes del año?
¿Cómo se llama el segundo mes del año?
¿Cómo se llama el tercer mes del año?
¿Cómo se llama el cuarto mes del año?
¿Cómo se llama el último mes del año?

¿Cuántos días tiene enero?
¿Cuántos días tiene febrero?
¿Cuántos días tiene marzo?
¿Cuántos días tiene abril?
¿Cuántos días tiene mayo?

marzo
abril
mayo

la primavera

La primavera es una estación del año.

junio
julio
agosto

el verano

El verano es otra estación del año.

septiembre
octubre
noviembre

el otoño

El otoño es otra estación del año.

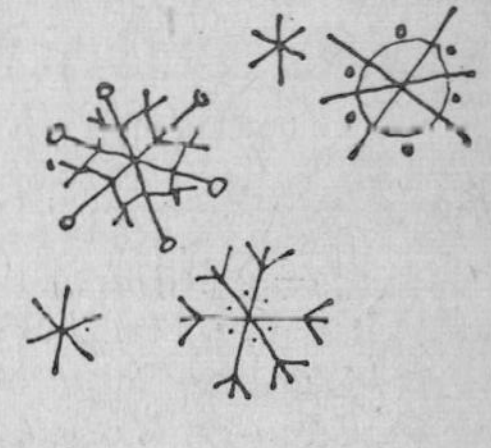

diciembre
enero
febrero

el invierno

El invierno es otra estación del año.

El año tiene cuatro estaciones.
Las estaciones del año son la primavera, el verano, el otoño y el invierno.

En la primavera hace un tiempo agradable.
Hace buen tiempo. Hace fresco. Hace sol.

En el verano hace calor. Hace mucho calor.

En el otoño hace un tiempo agradable.
Hace buen tiempo. Hace frío, pero no mucho.

En el invierno hace frío.
Hace mucho frío. Hace mal tiempo.

¿Qué tiempo hace hoy?

Hoy hace fresco. Hoy hace buen tiempo.

¿Qué tiempo hace hoy?

Hoy hace sol. Hace buen tiempo.

¿Qué tiempo hace hoy?

Hoy hace frío. No hace buen tiempo.

¿Qué tiempo hace hoy?

Hoy hace mal tiempo. Hace viento.
Hay polvo. Hay mucho polvo.

¿Qué tiempo hace hoy?

Hoy hace mal tiempo.
Está lloviendo. Llueve.

¿Qué tiempo hace hoy?

Hoy hace mal tiempo.
Está nevando. Nieva.

¿Qué tiempo hace hoy?

Hoy hace mal tiempo.
Hay lodo en las calles.
Hay mucho lodo en las calles.

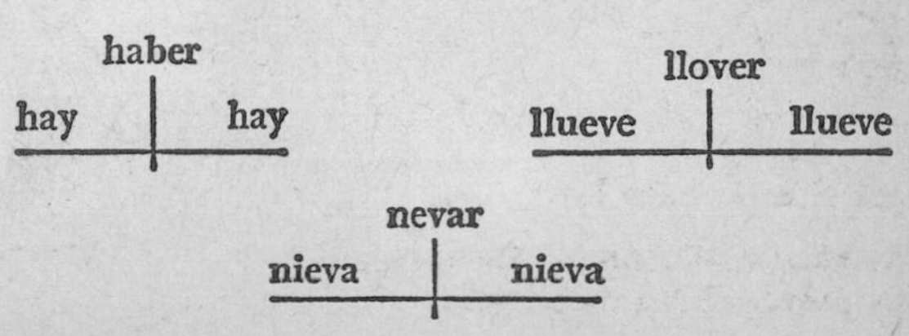

¿Le gusta la primavera, Elena?

Sí, me encanta, José. La primavera es la estación más agradable del año. Casi siempre hace buen tiempo. No hace ni frío ni calor. El aire es fresco y puro. Las plantas y los árboles están llenos de flores, y los pájaros cantan. Además, en la primavera no tengo ni frío ni calor porque no hace ni frío ni calor.

Sí, tiene razón; a mí también me encanta la primavera. Pero a veces llueve mucho, ¿no?

Sí, usted tiene razón; llueve de vez en cuando, pero yo no tengo miedo a la lluvia, siempre llevo conmigo un paraguas.

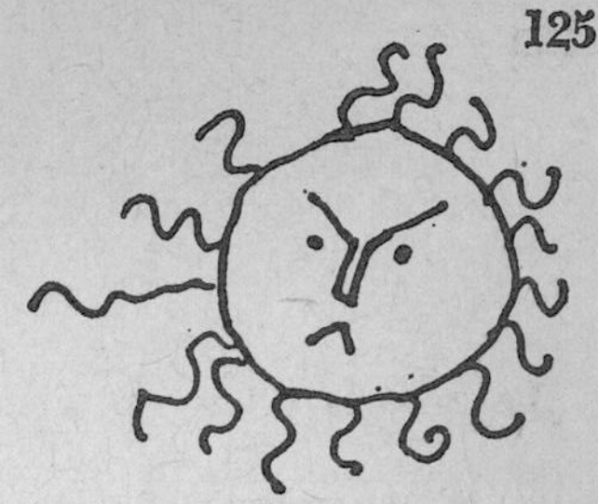

¿Le gustan las flores?

Sí, me encantan. A todo el mundo le gustan las flores, ¿no es verdad?

Sí, es verdad. ¿No le gusta el verano?

Me gusta cuando estoy en el campo, en las montañas, o en la playa, pero no me gusta cuando estoy en la ciudad. En el verano hace mejor tiempo que en el invierno. Los días son más largos; las noches son más cortas. Algunos días llueve mucho, y después de la lluvia hace humedad y hay mucho lodo en las calles. En el verano tenemos calor porque hace mucho calor. En el verano llevamos ropa ligera y clara para estar más frescos y cómodos. La ropa de seda o de algodón es muy fresca. En el verano tenemos mucha sed; tenemos ganas de beber.

En el otoño tampoco hace un tiempo agradable. Unas veces llueve, otras veces hace viento y hay polvo. A menudo el cielo está nublado, hay niebla y hace humedad. En el otoño llevamos un impermeable y un paraguas para andar en la lluvia.

En el invierno generalmente no hace un tiempo agradable. Hace peor tiempo que en el verano. Hace mucho frío, y muchas veces nieva. Los días son más cortos; las noches son más largas. En el invierno tenemos frío porque hace mucho frío. En el invierno llevamos ropa de abrigo para estar más abrigados. La ropa de lana abriga mucho, o da calor. En el invierno tenemos hambre; tenemos ganas de comer.

andar

ando	andamos
anda	andan

cantar

canto	cantamos
canta	cantan

llevar

llevo	llevamos
lleva	llevan

gustar

me gusta	nos gusta
me gustan	nos gustan
le gusta	les gusta
le gustan	les gustan

encantar

me encanta	nos encanta
me encantan	nos encantan
le encanta	les encanta
le encantan	les encantan

LAS PARTES DEL CUERPO HUMANO

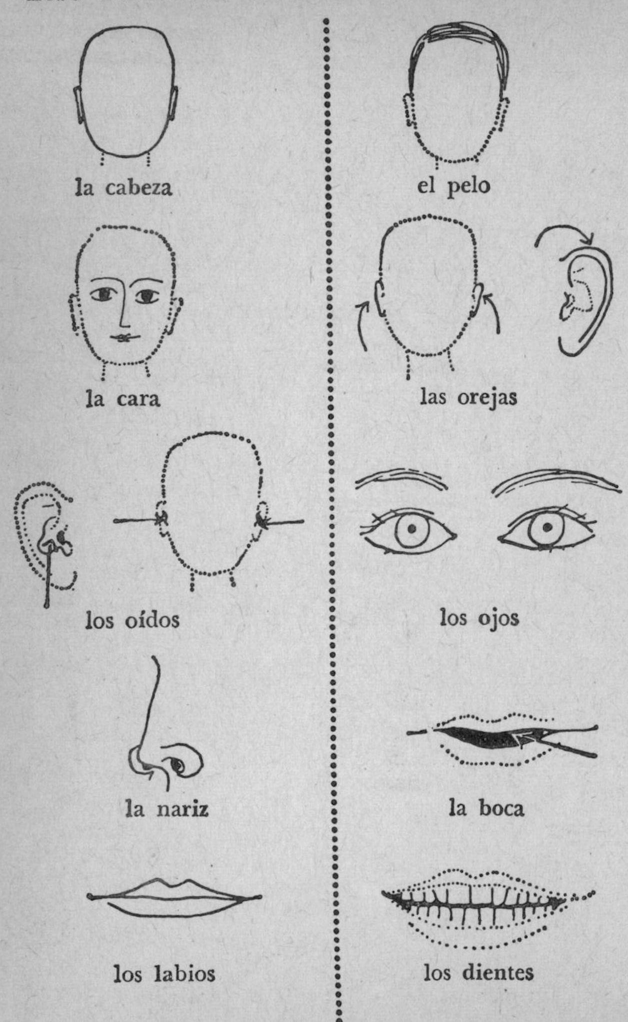

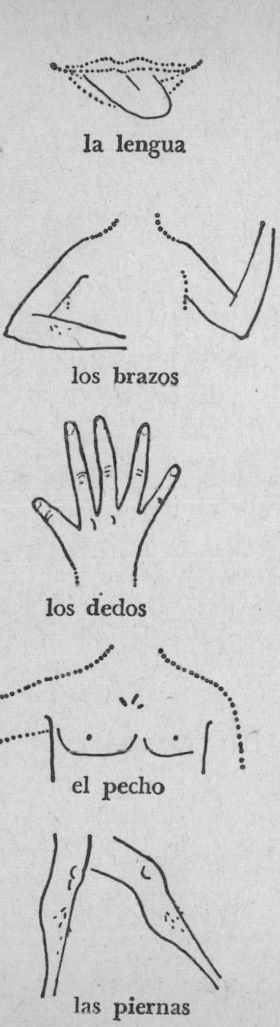

la lengua

los brazos

los dedos

el pecho

las piernas

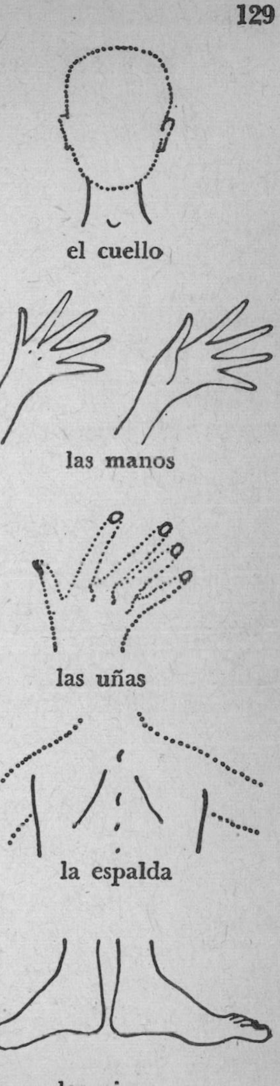

el cuello

las manos

las uñas

la espalda

los pies

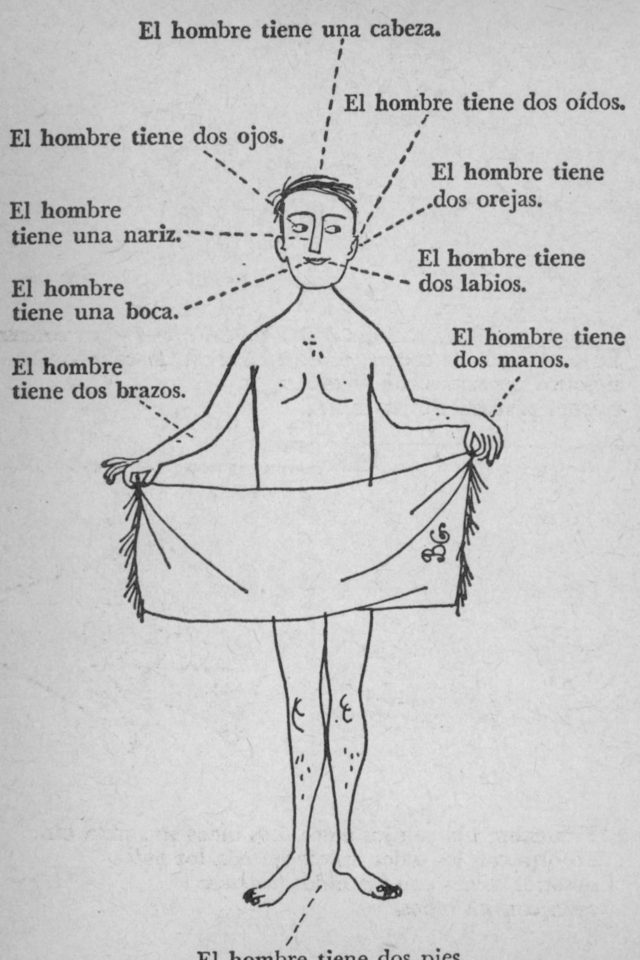
El hombre tiene una cabeza.
El hombre tiene dos oídos.
El hombre tiene dos ojos.
El hombre tiene dos orejas.
El hombre tiene una nariz.
El hombre tiene dos labios.
El hombre tiene una boca.
El hombre tiene dos manos.
El hombre tiene dos brazos.
El hombre tiene dos pies.

El hombre piensa con la cabeza. La cabeza es para pensar.
Yo pienso con la cabeza, usted piensa con la cabeza,
nosotros pensamos con la cabeza,
ustedes piensan con la cabeza.

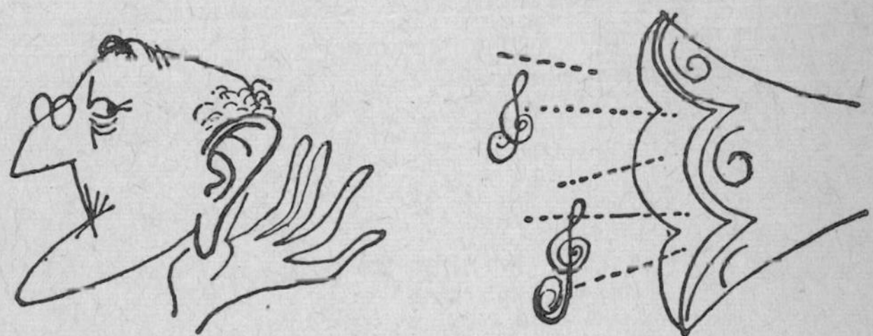

El hombre oye con los oídos. Los oídos son para oír.
Yo oigo con los oídos, usted oye con los oídos,
nosotros oímos con los oídos, ustedes
oyen con los oídos.

El hombre ve con los ojos. Los ojos son para ver. Yo veo con los ojos, usted ve con los ojos, nosotros vemos con los ojos, ustedes ven con los ojos.

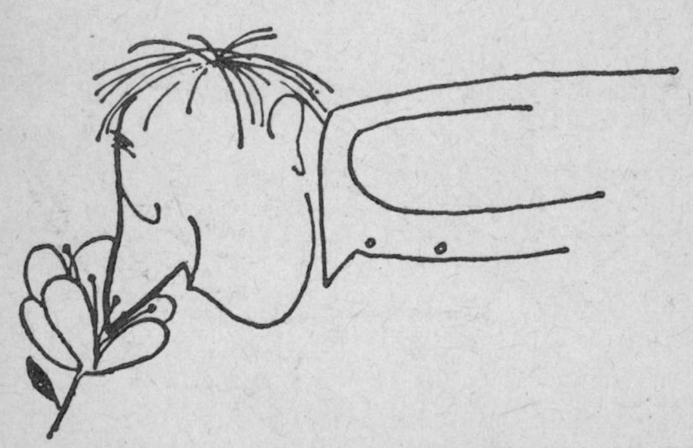

El hombre tiene una nariz. La nariz es para oler. Yo huelo con la nariz, usted huele con la nariz, nosotros olemos con la nariz, ustedes huelen con la nariz.

El hombre come con la boca. La boca es para comer. Yo como con la boca, usted come con la boca, nosotros comemos con la boca, ustedes comen con la boca.

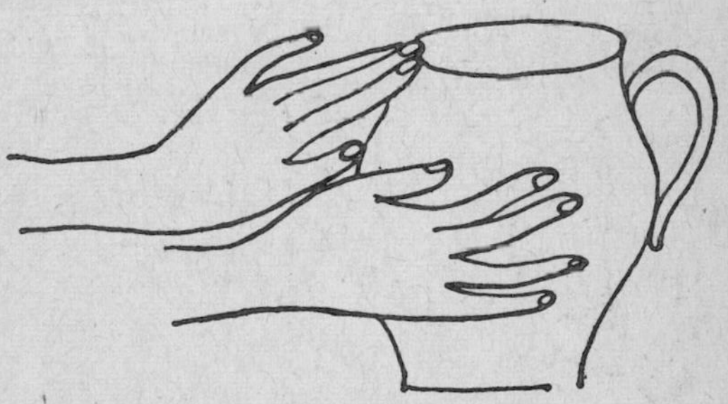

El hombre toca con las manos. Las manos son para tocar. Yo toco, usted toca, nosotros tocamos, ustedes tocan.

El hombre anda con los pies. Los pies son para andar. Yo ando, usted anda, nosotros andamos, ustedes andan.

El hombre besa con los labios. Los labios son para besar. Yo beso, usted besa, nosotros besamos, ustedes besan.

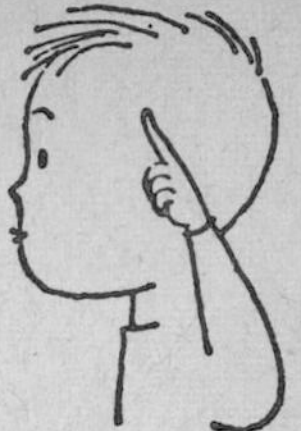

¿Para qué es la cabeza, Juanito?

La cabeza es para pensar.

¿En qué piensa usted ahora?

Pienso en mis estudios, en mi español, en mis padres, en mi hermana, y en muchas cosas.

¿Qué piensa hacer mañana?

Pienso leer, estudiar, y escribir a mis amigos.

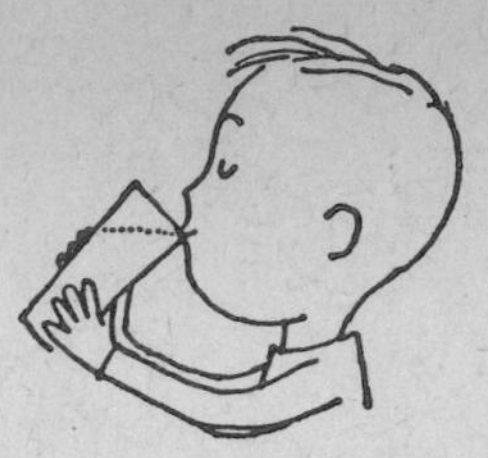

¿Para qué es la boca, Juanito?

La boca es para muchas cosas. La boca es, por ejemplo, para comer, beber, o tomar alimento. También es para hablar, preguntar, responder o contestar, y pedir favores o cosas.

¿Para qué son los ojos?

Los ojos son para ver y mirar.

¿Para qué es la nariz?

La nariz es para oler y respirar.

¿Para qué es la lengua?

La lengua es para hablar y también para probar alimentos.

¿Para qué son las orejas?

Las orejas no son para nada. Tal vez para adorno.

¿Para qué son los oídos?

Los oídos son para oír y escuchar.

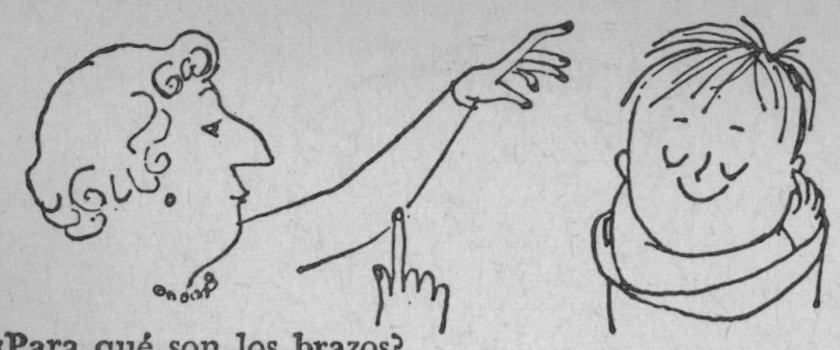

¿Para qué son los brazos?

Los brazos son para abrazar, y tambien para trabajar.

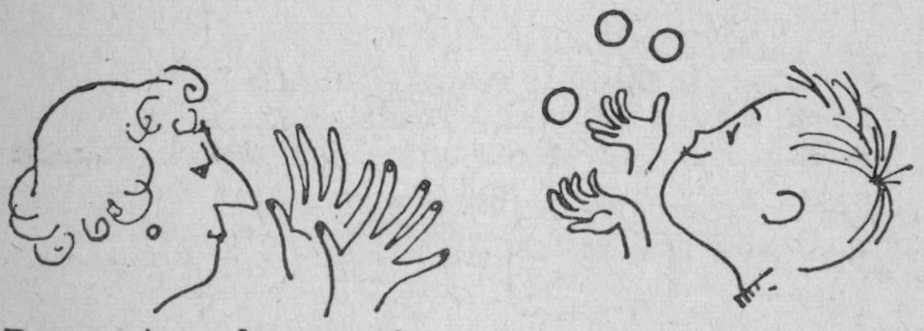

¿Para qué son las manos?

Las manos, como la boca, son para muchas cosas. Las manos son, por ejemplo, para trabajar, coger y tomar objetos; pero el empleo principal es para tocar.

¿Para qué son los pies?

Los pies son para andar o caminar, y para bailar.

A Juanito le duele la cabeza. Le duele la cabeza porque lee mucho. Juanito necesita un médico. Hay que buscar un médico. ¡Pobre Juanito!

A mí no me duele la cabeza, pero me duelen los ojos. Me duelen los ojos de tanto leer y estudiar. Tengo que descansar la vista.

¿Qué le duele, Guillermo?

Me duele un poco este brazo.

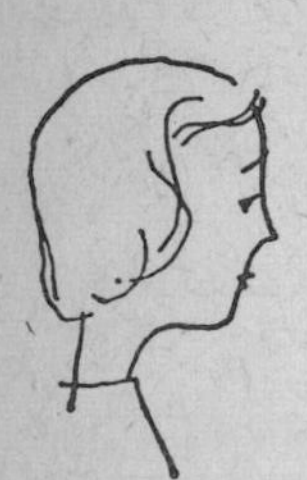

¿Le duelen las manos también?

No, las manos no me duelen.

¿Le duelen los pies?

No, tampoco me duelen los pies.

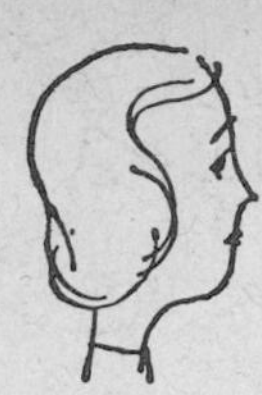

¿Qué le duele a usted?

A mí no me duele nada.

¡Qué suerte tiene usted!

necesitar

necesito	necesitamos
necesita	necesitan

doler

me duele mc duelen	nos duele nos duelen
le duele le duelen	les duele les duelen

Juanito tiene los ojos y el pelo negros. Juanito es moreno.

¿Es rubio Juanito?

¿De qué color tiene Juanito los ojos y el pelo?

Su hermana, Anita, tiene los ojos azules y el pelo rubio. Ella es rubia.

¿Es morena su hermana?

¿De qué color tiene Anita los ojos y el pelo?

¿Qué tiene usted en la mano derecha?

Tengo un libro en la mano derecha.

¿Qué tiene usted en la mano izquierda?

No tengo nada en la mano izquierda.

¿Qué tienen los niños en la mano derecha?

Tienen varios libros en la mano derecha.

¿Qué tienen los niños en la boca?

Tienen dulces en la boca.

UN DÍA EN LA VIDA DEL SEÑOR ADAMS

POR LA MAÑANA

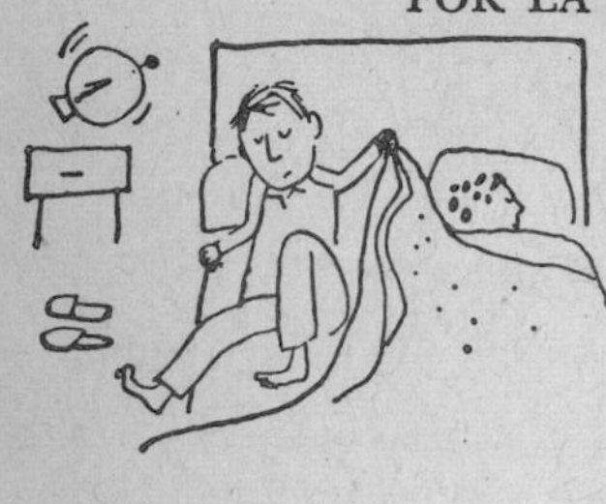

Me despierto a las 7:30 y me levanto a las 7:35.

Juanito, mi hijo, se despierta a las 7:40 y se levanta a las 7:45.

Mi mujer y mi hija se despiertan a las 8:00 y se levantan a las 8:15.

Después de levantarme voy al cuarto de baño.

Cuando estoy en el cuarto de baño me lavo las manos y la cara con agua caliente o fría y jabón.

Me seco las manos y la cara con una toalla.

despertarse

me despierto	nos despertamos
se despierta	se despiertan

lavarse

me lavo	nos lavamos
se lava	se lavan

secarse

me seco	nos secamos
se seca	se secan

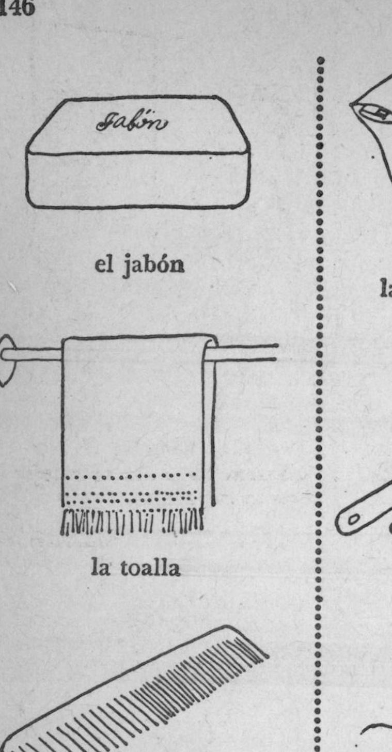

el jabón

la toalla

el peine

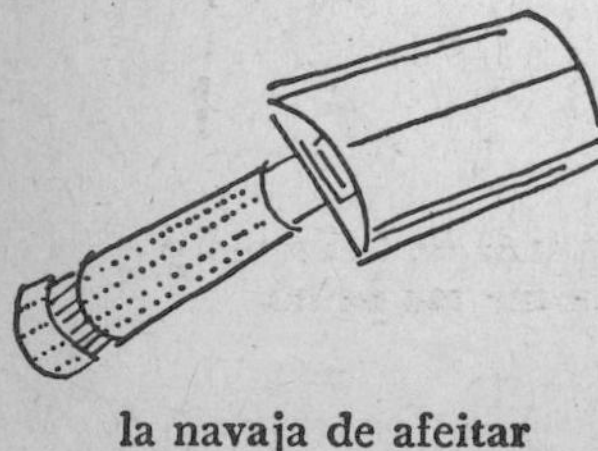

la navaja de afeitar

la pasta de dientes

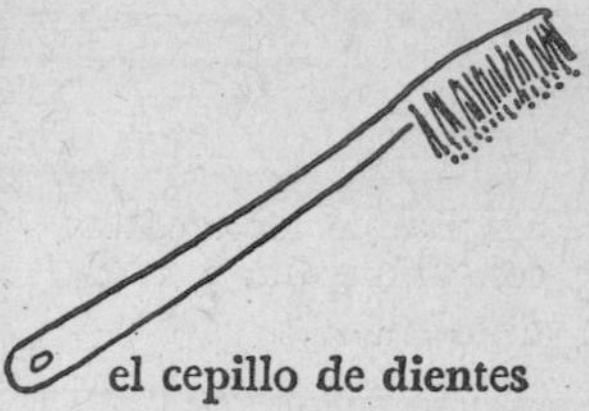

el cepillo de dientes

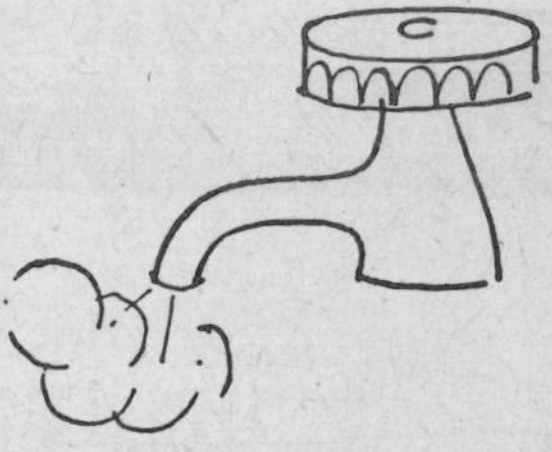

el agua caliente

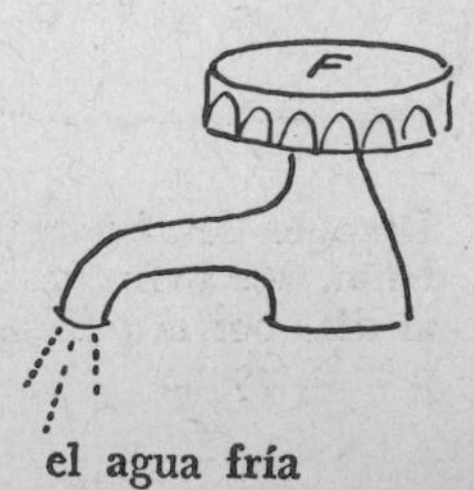

el agua fría

Me limpio los dientes con un cepillo y pasta de dientes.

Me afeito todas las mañanas. Me miro al espejo cuando me afeito.

Después de afeitarme me baño. Me baño dos veces al día: por la mañana y por la noche.

Después de bañarme y secarme me peino.

limpiarse

me limpio	nos limpiamos
se limpia	se limpian

afeitarse

me afeito	nos afeitamos
se afeita	se afeitan

bañarse

me baño	nos bañamos
se baña	se bañan

peinarse

me peino	nos peinamos
se peina	se peinan

mirarse

me miro	nos miramos
se mira	se miran

Nosotros nos despertamos y nos
levantamos a diferentes horas.
Yo me despierto temprano.
Mis hijos se despiertan tarde.
Me lavo con agua caliente y jabón.
Me seco las manos con una toalla.
En mi casa nos bañamos todos los días.
Me peino. Me miro al espejo.

¿A qué hora se despierta usted?
¿A qué hora se despiertan ellos?
¿A qué hora se levanta usted?
¿A qué hora se levantan los niños?
¿Se lava usted con agua fría?
¿Con qué nos limpiamos los dientes?
¿Con qué nos secamos las manos?
¿Se baña usted con agua fría?
¿Con qué se peina usted?
¿Para qué se mira usted al espejo?

LA ROPA

el sombrero

la gorra

la camisa

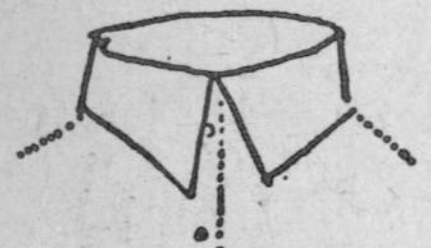
el cuello

la corbata

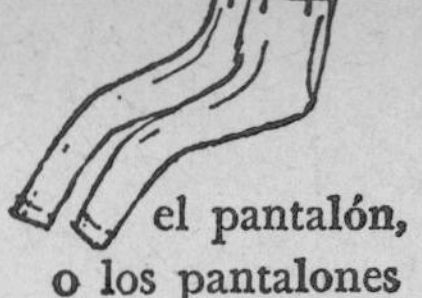
el pantalón,
o los pantalones

el chaleco

la chaqueta, o el saco

el pañuelo

el traje

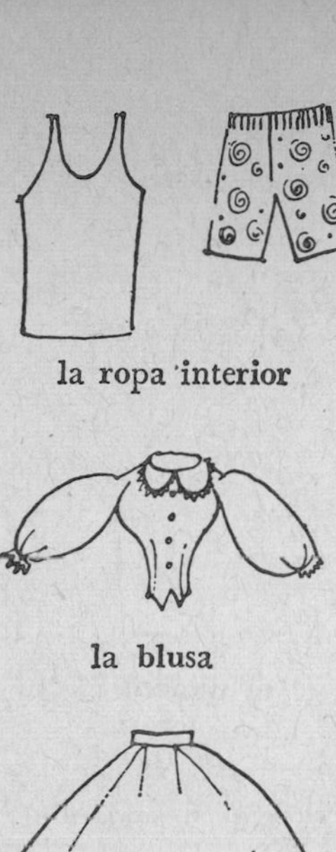

la ropa interior

la blusa

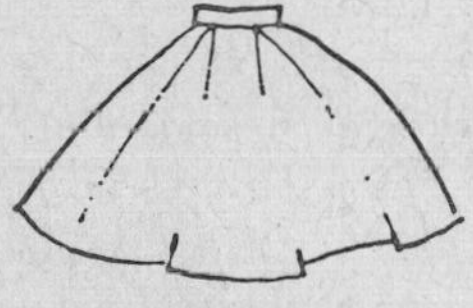

la falda

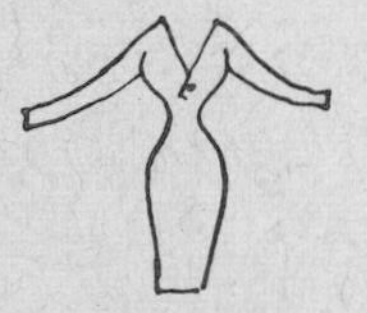

el vestido

las medias

el abrigo, o el sobretodo

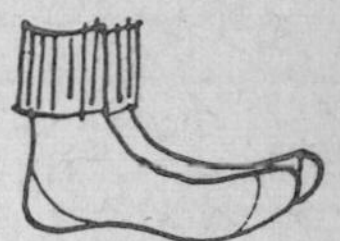

los calcetines

el suéter

los zapatos

los guantes

Después de lavarme, afeitarme, bañarme, secarme y peinarme me visto.

Mi hijo no se afeita, pero se lava, se baña, se seca, se peina y se viste lo mismo que yo.

El hombre se pone el pantalón, los calcetines, los zapatos, la camisa, la corbata, y la chaqueta.

La mujer se pone la falda, la blusa, las medias, los zapatos, y el sombrero cuando sale a la calle.

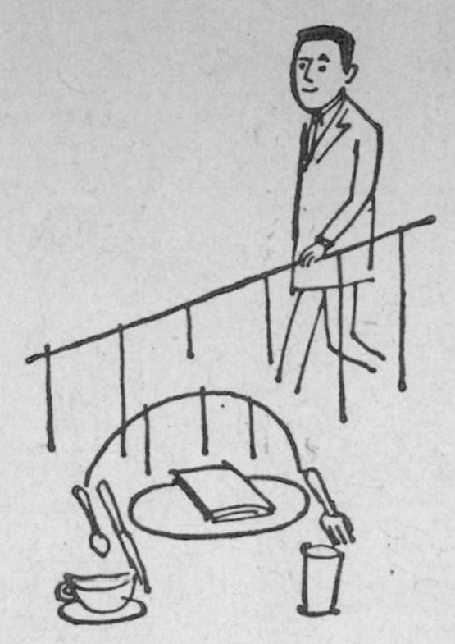

Después de vestirme bajo al comedor para desayunarme.

Me siento a la mesa para tomar el desayuno.

vestirse

me visto	nos vestimos
se viste	se visten

desayunarse

me desayuno	nos desayunamos
se desayuna	se desayunan

bajar

bajo	bajamos
baja	bajan

EL DESAYUNO

una naranja
el jugo de naranja

una toronja
media toronja

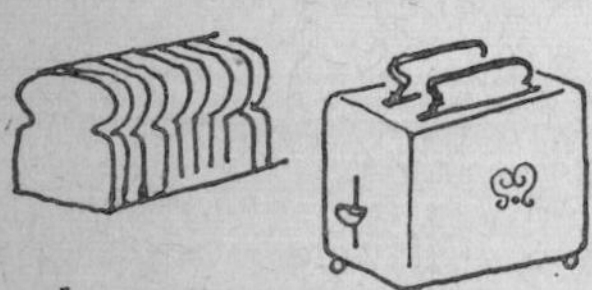

el pan
el pan tostado

la mantequilla

el azúcar

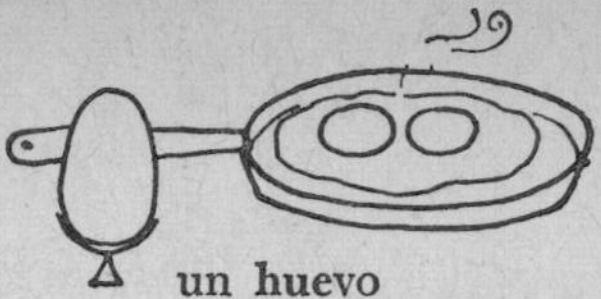

un huevo
los huevos fritos

huevos pasados por agua
(3 minutos)

el jamón, el tocino

una taza de café

la leche
un vaso de leche

Mi desayuno consiste en un jugo de naranja, huevos fritos con jamón, pan tostado con mantequilla y una taza de café solo. Me gusta el café sin azúcar y sin leche.

Cuando acabo el desayuno me levanto de la mesa y me preparo para ir a mi despacho. Es decir, me pongo el abrigo, los guantes y el sombrero.

Si hace buen tiempo voy a pie. Yo tardo solamente quince minutos de mi casa a mi despacho. Mi despacho no está lejos de mi casa.

Si hace mal tiempo tomo el autobús en la calle 70 y avenida Mádison. El autobús pasa por esa avenida. Hay una parada en la esquina de la calle 70 y la avenida Mádison.

Me bajo en la calle 57. El autobús va directo a la calle 57 y Mádison. No tengo que cambiar de autobús.

Cuando me bajo del autobús vuelvo a la derecha. Ando una cuadra para llegar al edificio en que está mi despacho. Mi despacho está a una cuadra del lugar en que me bajo.

acabar

acabo	acabamos
acaba	acaban

prepararse

me preparo	nos preparamos
se prepara	se preparan

cambiar

cambio	cambiamos
cambia	cambian

pasar

paso	pasamos
pasa	pasan

tardar

tardo	tardamos
tarda	tardan

Tardo quince minutos en llegar a mi despacho.
El autobús tarda mucho en llegar.
Nosotros no tardamos mucho en prepararnos.
El autobús no pasa por esta calle.
Tomo el autobús en esta esquina.
Acabo mi trabajo a las 4:30.
No tengo que cambiar de autobús para ir a mi oficina.

¿Cuánto tiempo tarda usted en llegar a su casa?
¿Cuánto tiempo tarda el autobús?
¿Cuánto tiempo tardan ustedes en prepararse?
¿Pasa por aquí el autobús?
¿Dónde toma usted el autobús?
¿A qué hora acaban ustedes su trabajo?
¿Tenemos que cambiar de autobús para ir a Wáshington?

Cuando llego a mi despacho me quito los guantes y los meto en el bolsillo del abrigo.

Luego me quito el sombrero y el abrigo y los cuelgo.

Me siento al escritorio y saco la llavc del bolsillo del pantalón para abrir el cajón del escritorio.

Telefoneo a varios clientes y amigos, y leo las últimas noticias en el periódico.

meter	
meto	metemos
mete	meten

colgar	
cuelgo	colgamos
cuelga	cuelgan

sacar	
saco	sacamos
saca	sacan

telefonear	
telefoneo	telefoneamos
telefonea	telefonean

A la una tengo hambre y sed. Al otro lado de la calle hay un restaurante muy bueno y barato. Cruzo la calle para ir al restaurante.

Al entrar, el camarero me da las buenas tardes y me indica una mesa que hay al lado de una ventana. La ventana da a la calle.

En la mesa hay un plato, una
servilleta, un cuchillo,
una cuchara, una cucharita, un tenedor,
un vaso para el agua y una copa para el vino.

Llamo al camarero y le pido la lista de platos.
El camarero me da la lista. ¿Me hace usted el
favor de tomar la orden? Es tarde y tengo mucha prisa.

LISTA DE PLATOS

ALMUERZO

la sopa
sopa de legumbres

el pollo
pollo a la parrilla

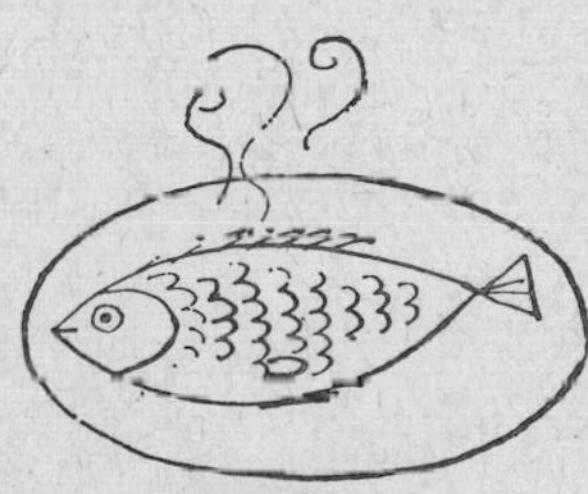

el pescado

el emparedado

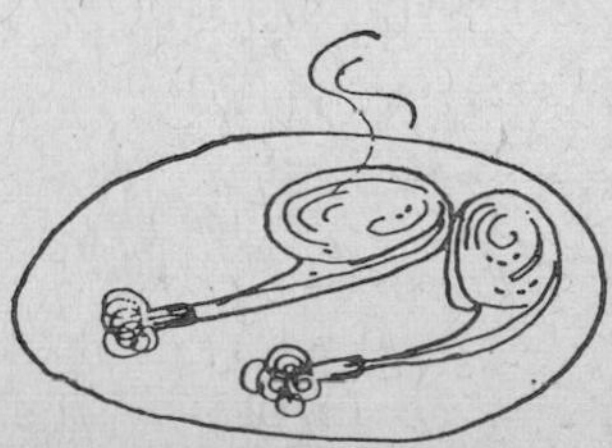

las costillas de cordero

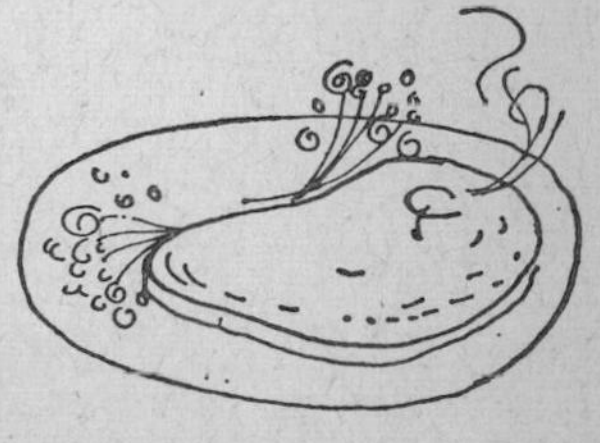

el biftec

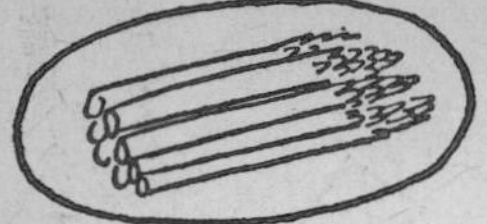

las legumbres:
los espárragos

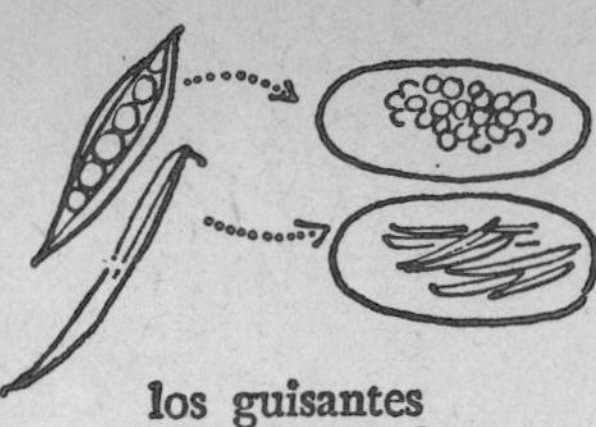

los guisantes
las habichuelas

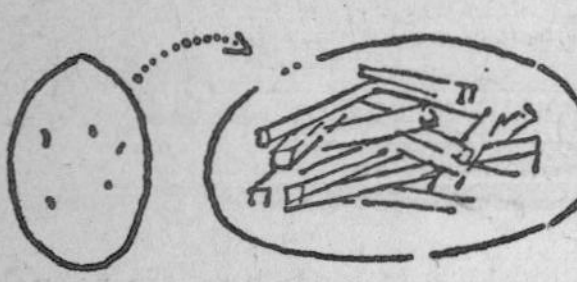

las patatas
fritas

el queso

la ensalada de
lechuga y tomate

la manzana

postres:
el helado de chocolate

la pera
las uvas

¿Qué quiere tomar, caballero?

Quiero pescado, espárragos, patatas fritas, ensalada de lechuga y tomate, fruta y una taza de café.

Camarero, ¿hace usted el favor de traerme la cuenta?

En seguida señor, aquí la tiene usted.

¿Pago a usted, o pago en la caja?

En la caja, gracias.

El camarero me trae el cambio; le dejo una propina en la mesa, y vuelvo a mi despacho.

cruzar

cruzo	cruzamos
cruza	cruzan

pedir

pido	pedimos
pide	piden

querer

quiero	queremos
quiere	quieren

traer

traigo	traemos
trae	traen

pagar

pago	pagamos
paga	pagan

dejar

dejo	dejamos
deja	dejan

Tengo mucha hambre.
En esta calle hay un buen restaurante.
No tenemos que cruzar la calle para ir allí.
Este cuarto da a la calle.
Me gusta la sopa muy caliente,
pero esta sopa está fría.
Yo pido pescado y mi amigo pide carne.
Hoy no quiero tomar vino.
Pago la cuenta al camarero.
El camarero trae el cambio al señor.

¿Tiene usted mucha sed?
¿Dónde hay un buen restaurante?
¿Qué tenemos que hacer para ir al restaurante?
¿A dónde da este cuarto?
¿Le gusta el café muy caliente?
¿Quién pide pescado?
¿Quién pide carne?
Si usted no quiere tomar vino, ¿qué quiere tomar?
¿Cuánto deja de propina?

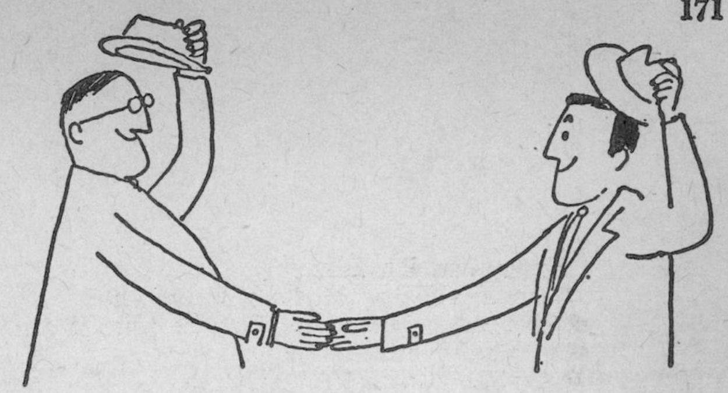

Buenas tardes, querido amigo.

Muy buenas, don Francisco. Me alegro mucho de verle.

Al salir del despacho el señor Adams se encuentra con un amigo. Al saludarse se dan la mano.

¿Cómo está la familia?

La mujer y la niña están bien, pero el niño se encuentra un poco enfermo. No es nada serio, ¡gracias a Dios!

El amigo pregunta a don Francisco por la salud de su familia.

¿Ya sabe usted el día que sale para México?

Todavía no lo sé. Tal vez un día del mes que viene.

¿Va usted por mucho tiempo?

Vamos por una semana.

¡Ah! ¿va la familia tambien?

Desde luego. Vamos todos.

¡Qué lástima! ¿No pueden ir por más de una semana?

Yo no puedo. Mi mujer quiere ir por un mes, pero mis asuntos no me permiten ir por más tiempo.

¿Sabe usted hablar bien el español?

No, no lo sé hablar ni bien ni mal. Mis hijos lo saben bastante bien, pero mi mujer y yo no lo hablamos.

¿Puede usted decirme la hora que es?

Sí, son las 5:15.

¡Las 5:15 ya! Perdóneme, pero tengo que correr si no quiero llegar tarde a mi casa. Mi mujer espera visita. ¿Quiere usted acompañarme?

No puedo, muchas gracias.

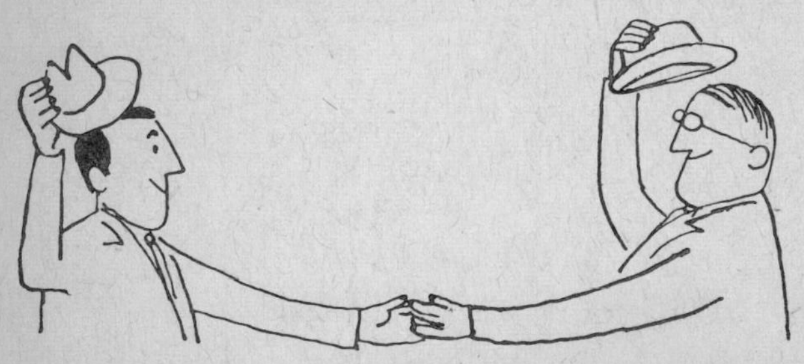

Entonces, adiós, querido amigo. Hasta muy pronto.

Adiós, don Francisco. ¡Buen viaje!

alegrarse

me alegro	nos alegramos
se alegra	se alegran

encontrarse

me encuentro	nos encontramos
se encuentra	se encuentran

saber

sé	sabemos
sabe	saben

preguntar

pregunto	preguntamos
pregunta	preguntan

permitir

permito	permitimos
permite	permiten

poder

puedo	podemos
puede	pueden

Hoy me encuentro un poco enfermo.
Mis hijos se encuentran bien.
Me encuentro con mis amigos al salir de casa.
José me pregunta si sé la dirección de Guillermo.
Ellos no saben que voy a México.
No sé la hora que es.
Ella no puede ir este año.
Nosotros tampoco podemos ir.
Me alegro de verla, María.
El mal tiempo no nos permite salir.

¿Cómo se encuentra usted hoy?
¿Se encuentran sus hijos bien?
¿Con quién se encuentra usted al salir de casa?
¿Qué le pregunta José?
¿Sabe usted la dirección de la señorita Winter?
¿Saben ustedes cómo se llama el presidente de los Estados Unidos?
¿Quién no puede ir a México este año?
¿Se alegran ustedes de ir a Europa?
¿Qué no nos permite salir?

Buenas tardes, Francisco. ¿Está Elena en casa?

Buenas tardes, María. Sí, está en la sala. Pase usted.

María viene a visitar a los Adams.

¿No quiere usted una copa de vino de Jerez antes de pasar a la sala?

Sí, gracias. Me gusta mucho el vino de Jerez.

Francisco ofrece una copa de Jerez a María.

Señorita Cruz, el señor García.

Mucho gusto, señor García.

Tanto gusto en conocerla, señorita Cruz.

El señor Adams presenta el señor García a la señorita Cruz. Ellos no se conocen.

Señor Ibarra, el señor García.

Mucho gusto en conocerle, señor García.

Encantado, señor Ibarra.

El señor Adams presenta el señor García al señor Ibarra. Ellos tampoco se conocen.

Señora de Cervantes, ¿conoce usted a la señora de García?

No, no tengo ese placer. Mucho gusto en conocerla, señora de García.

El gusto es mío, señora de Cervantes.

Ustedes se conocen, ¿verdad?

Si, ¿cómo está usted, señor Dalton?

Mucho gusto en verle otra vez señor García.

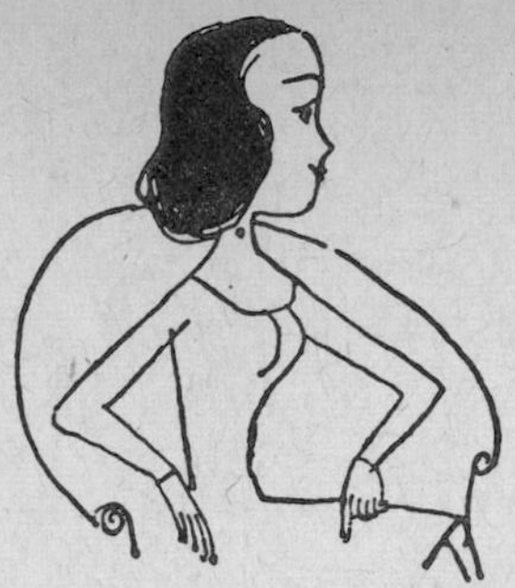

¿Hace mucho tiempo que está usted en Nueva York, señora de García?

Sí, hace mucho tiempo; hace dos años que mi marido y yo estamos aquí.

¿Hace mucho tiempo que estudia usted el español, señor Dalton?

Hace año y medio que lo estudio.

¿Hace mucho tiempo que conoce usted al señor Dalton, señor García?

Hace tres meses que le conozco.

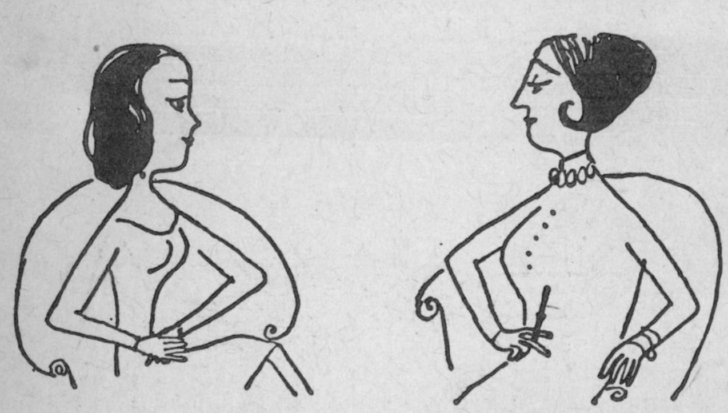

¿Hace mucho tiempo que no va usted a Venezuela?

Hace tres años que no voy a Venezuela.

¿Hace mucho tiempo que no ve usted a María?

Hace solamente una semana que no la veo.

¿Hace mucho tiempo que no sabe usted de sus padres?

Hace un mes que no sé de ellos.

¿Desde cuándo no ve usted a María?

No la veo desde anoche.

¿Desde cuándo no sabe usted de sus padres?

No sé de ellos desde la semana pasada.

¿Desde cuándo no lleva sombrero?

No llevo sombrero desde junio.

¿Desde cuándo trabaja usted para esa casa?

Desde el año pasado.

pasar

paso	pasamos
pasa	pasan

presentar

presento	presentamos
presenta	presentan

ofrecer

ofrezco	ofrecemos
ofrece	ofrecen

conocer

conozco	conocemos
conoce	conocen

Elena está en la sala.
María pasa a la sala.
María viene a visitar a sus amigos.
María no conoce al señor García.
El señor Adams presenta el señor
García a la señorita Cruz.
El señor Adams los presenta.
La señora de Cervantes y la señora
de García no se conocen.
El señor Adams las presenta.
Hace un año que no voy a España.
Hace mucho tiempo que ellos no ven a María.
Yo no veo a Elena desde Enero.
Yo no escribo a mis padres desde
la semana pasada.

¿Dónde está Elena?
¿A dónde pasa María?
¿A qué viene María?
¿Conoce María al señor García?
¿Quién presenta el señor García a
la señorita Cruz?
¿Conoce usted a la señorita Cruz?
¿Se conocen la señora de Cervantes
y la señora de García?
¿Quién las presenta?
¿Cuánto tiempo hace que no va usted a España?
¿Cuánto tiempo hace que ellos no ven a María?
¿Desde cuándo no ve usted a Elena?
¿Desde cuándo no escribe usted a sus padres?

POR LA NOCHE

Elena está muy alegre y muy contenta. Sus amigos son tan simpáticos, tan finos, tan encantadores, y tan corteses.

Después de despedirse de sus amigos, Elena va a la cocina. Ella está ahora en la cocina. Prepara la cena para la familia.

El señor Adams está en la alcoba. Hace la maleta para el viaje. Trata de meter en la maleta toda la ropa, pero no es fácil, la ropa no cabe en una maleta.

Juanito trata de ayudar a su padre. Trata de meter los libros en el bolsillo del abrigo. Los libros no caben en él. El bolsillo es más pequeño que los libros, y por eso no caben.

Entonces Juanito trata de meter en la cartera los libros. La cartera es grande, por lo tanto los libros caben en ella.

Elena sirve la comida. La comida está servida. Ella llama a su marido y a sus niños.

Después de la cena el señor Adams va a la biblioteca. Quiere escribir unas cartas importantes antes de acostarse.

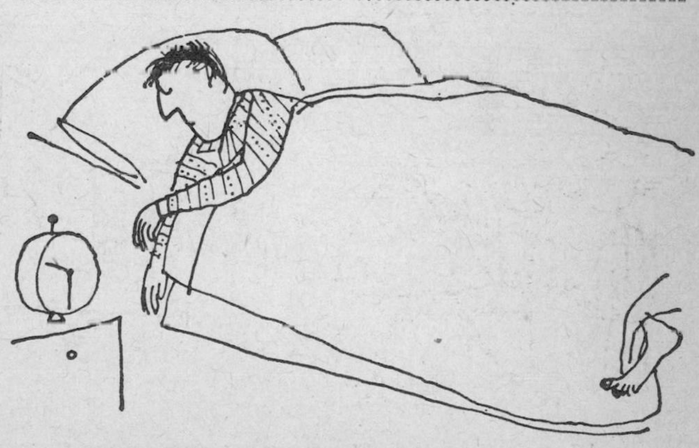

Se acuesta a las 10:30. Se acuesta temprano porque quiere dormir ocho horas por lo menos. Él no duerme bien.

tratar

trato	tratamos
trata	tratan

caber

quepo	cabemos
cabe	caben

acostarse

me acuesto	nos acostamos
se acuesta	se acuestan

dormir

duermo	dormimos
duerme	duermen

ayudar

ayudo	ayudamos
ayuda	ayudan

servir

sirvo	servimos
sirve	sirven

Elena no está triste, está alegre.
Ella prepara la cena para la familia.
Yo no quepo en este asiento.
En este cuarto caben diez personas.
El sombrero no cabe en la maleta.
Juanito trata de ayudar a su padre.
Yo me acuesto tarde.
Esta noche quiero acostarme temprano.
Los niños no se acuestan tarde.
Ellos duermen muy bien.
Yo no duermo muy bien.

¿Por qué está alegre Elena?
¿Para quién prepara ella la cena?
¿Por qué no quepo yo en este asiento?
¿Cuántas personas caben en este cuarto?
¿Qué no cabe en la maleta?
¿A quién trata de ayudar Juanito?
¿A qué hora se acuesta usted?
¿A qué hora quiere acostarse esta noche?
¿A qué hora se acuestan los niños?
¿Duermen mal los niños?
¿Quién no duerme muy bien?

Yo veo a Guillermo.
Yo lo veo.
(o, Yo le veo.)

Veo a María.
La veo.

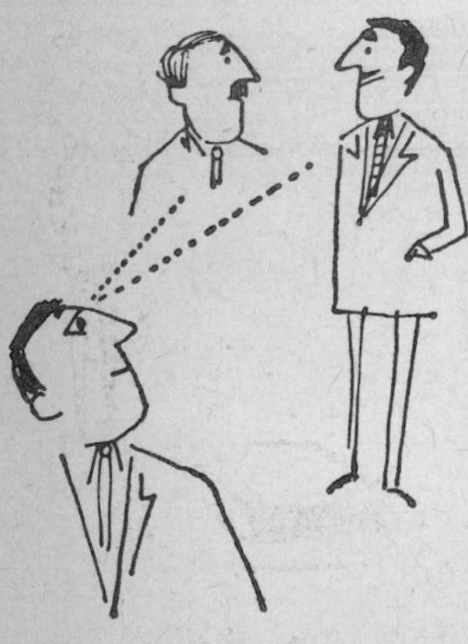

Veo a Guillermo y a José.
Los veo.

Veo a María y a Elena.
Las veo.

Veo a Guillermo y a María.
Los veo.

María me ve.
Me ve.

María nos ve.
Nos ve.

Veo el libro.
Lo veo.

Veo la silla.
La veo.

Veo los libros.
Los veo.

Veo las sillas.
Las veo.

Veo los libros y las sillas. Los veo.

Yo veo a mi padre, a mi madre, a mi hermana, a María, a Guillermo, al profesor, al señor Juárez, a la señora de Cervantes, a los hijos del señor García y a las hermanas dc Carolina. Yo los veo a todos.

Yo veo el libro, las flores, la chaqueta, los guantes, los zapatos, la corbata y el paraguas. Yo los veo todos.

Yo quiero a una mujer y a dos muchachos. Esa mujer es mi esposa, y los muchachos son mis hijos. Yo los quiero mucho.

Yo quiero una mujer y dos muchachos.
Los quiero para trabajar en mi oficina.

Yo tengo una mujer encantadora.
Esa mujer es mi esposa.

Yo tengo una secretaria muy inteligente.

Señor Adams, ¿conoce usted al señor García?

Sí, lo conozco muy bien.
(o, Sí, le conozco muy bien.)

Juanito, ¿sabe usted cómo se dice *good morning* en español?

Sí, lo sé muy bien. Se dice buenos días.

Yo doy el libro a José.
Yo le doy el libro. (o, Yo le doy el libro a José.)

Yo doy el libro a usted.
Yo le doy el libro. (o, Yo le doy el libro a usted.)

Yo doy el libro a él.
Yo le doy el libro. (o, Yo le doy el libro a él.)

Yo doy el libro a ella.
Yo le doy el libro. (o, Yo le doy el libro a ella.)

Yo doy el libro a ustedes.
Yo les doy el libro. (o, Yo les doy el libro a ustedes.)

Yo doy el libro a ellos.
Yo les doy el libro. (o, Yo les doy el libro a ellos.)

Yo doy el libro a ellas.
Yo les doy el libro. (o, Yo les doy el libro a ellas.)

Yo doy el libro a María y a José.
Yo les doy el libro. (o, Yo les doy el libro a María y a José.)

Él me da el libro. (o, Él me da el libro a mí.)

Él nos da el libro. (o, Él nos da el libro a nosotros.)

Yo doy los libros a usted. Yo se los doy. (o, Yo se los doy a usted.)

Yo doy los libros a él. Yo se los doy. (o, Yo se los doy a él.)

Yo doy los libros a ella.
Yo se los doy. (o, Yo
se los doy a ella.)

Yo doy los libros a José.
Yo se los doy. (o, Yo
se los doy a José.)

Yo doy los libros a ustedes.
Yo se los doy. (o, Yo
se los doy a ustedes.)

Yo doy los libros a ellos.
Yo se los doy. (o, Yo
se los doy a ellos.)

Yo doy los libros a ellas.
Yo se los doy. (o, Yo
se los doy a ellas.)

Yo doy los libros a María
y a José. Yo se los doy.
(o, Yo se los doy a María
y a José.)

Él me da los libros.
Él me los da. (o, Él
me los da a mí.)

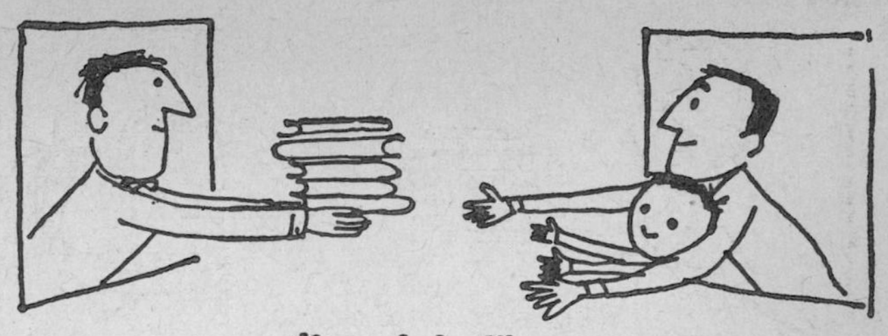

Él nos da los libros.
Él nos los da. (o, Él nos los da a nosotros.)

José no da el libro a él, sino a ella. José no se lo da a él, sino a ella.

Guillermo no me da el libro a mí, sino a María. Guillermo no me lo da a mí, sino a María.

¿Dónde ve usted a Guillermo?
¿A quiénes ve usted?
¿Qué ve usted?
¿Va usted al cine con su amiga?
¿Escribe usted con mi pluma?
¿De quién habla usted?
¿De qué habla usted?
¿A quién quiere usted?
¿Qué quiere usted, señor?
¿Tienen ustedes hijos?
¿A quién le da usted el libro?
¿Quién le da el libro a usted?
¿Da usted los libros a María o a José?

Lo veo en la sala.
Veo a Guillermo y a José.
Veo la ciudad desde esta ventana.
Sí, voy con ella.
Sí, escribo con ella.
Hablo de la señorita Cruz.
Hablo del idioma español.
Quiero a mis padres.
Quiero un profesor para estudiar el español.
Sí, tenemos dos.
Se lo doy a este señor.
Usted me lo da.
Se los doy a María.

hablar:	*comer:*	*vivir:*
hablo	como	vivo
habla	come	vive
hablamos	comemos	vivimos
hablan	comen	viven

Yo hablo español.
Yo hablo bien el español.
Yo hablo siempre en español con mi profesor.
Mi padre come en casa.
Mi padre come en casa todos los días.
Ellos viven en una casa blanca.
Ellos viven en una casa blanca, grande y nueva.
Él no trabaja hoy.
Él nunca trabaja los sábados y los domingos.
Él no trabaja nunca los sábados y los domingos.
¿Dónde pongo los libros?
¿Quiere usted venir conmigo?
Yo no puedo hacer eso ahora.
Usted debe estudiar más.
Hay muchas personas en la sala.
Hay que terminar el trabajo.
Acabo de leer este libro.

Hace poco tiempo que estudio el español.
Hace una semana que no escribo a mis padres.
María va a comprar un vestido para el viaje.
Yo voy a estudiar mi lección.
Por poco compro el automóvil.

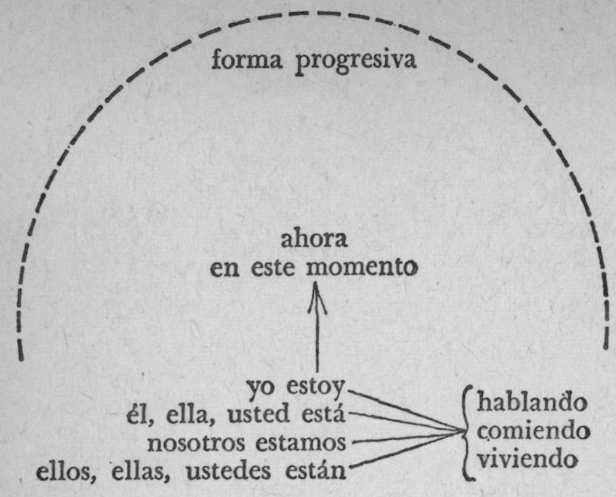

¿Qué está haciendo usted ahora, Juanito?
Estoy hablando con mi padre.

¿Están ustedes comiendo?
No, estamos estudiando y escribiendo las lecciones para mañana.

¿Dónde está su hermana?
Está lavándose las manos.

Forma habitual, no forma progresiva:

¿A dónde va usted, Juanito?
Voy a mi casa.

¿De dónde viene usted, Juanito?
Vengo de mi casa.

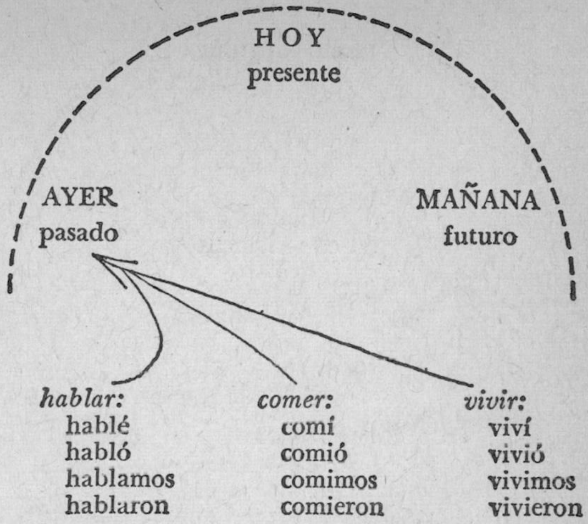

hablar:	*comer:*	*vivir:*
hablé	comí	viví
habló	comió	vivió
hablamos	comimos	vivimos
hablaron	comieron	vivieron

Yo hablé ayer en español con mi profesor.
Usted habló esta mañana acerca de su viaje a Sud América.
Ellos comieron tarde anoche.
Ustedes vivieron cinco años en el Perú.
Ellos salieron más temprano que ustedes.
María llegó tarde a su casa.
Yo no fui abogado, fui profesor de español.
Yo no fui a casa de mis amigos, fui a mi casa.

Elena, ¿vio usted a los niños?
Sí, los vi en la sala hace un momento.

¿Dio usted los billetes a José?
Sí, se los di hace ocho días.

¿Hubo mucho trabajo hoy?
Sí, hubo mucho trabajo y también hubo muchas cosas que hacer.

Ayer estuve estudiando todo el día.

andar:	*estar:*	*pedir:*	*sentir:*
anduve	estuve	pedí	sentí
anduvo	estuvo	pidió	sintió
anduvimos	estuvimos	pedimos	sentimos
anduvieron	estuvieron	pidieron	sintieron
caber:	*hacer:*	*poder:*	*ser:*
cupe	hice	pude	fui
cupo	hizo	pudo	fue
cupimos	hicimos	pudimos	fuimos
cupieron	hicieron	pudieron	fueron
dar:	*ir:*	*poner:*	*tener:*
di	fui	puse	tuve
dio	fue	puso	tuvo
dimos	fuimos	pusimos	tuvimos
dieron	fueron	pusieron	tuvieron
decir:	*leer:*	*querer:*	*traer:*
dije	leí	quise	traje
dijo	leyó	quiso	trajo
dijimos	leímos	quisimos	trajimos
dijeron	leyeron	quisieron	trajeron
dormir:	*oír:*	*saber:*	*venir:*
dormí	oí	supe	vine
durmió	oyó	supo	vino
dormimos	oímos	supimos	vinimos
durmieron	oyeron	supieron	vinieron

Yo anduve todo el día por las calles de la ciudad y ahora estoy cansado.

Los zapatos no cupieron en la maleta y tuve que meterlos en una caja.

Ellos no me dieron la caja a mí, sino a mi mujer.

Ellos no estuvieron nunca en México, pero piensan ir este año.

Yo no dormí bien anoche debido al calor, pero los niños durmieron diez horas.

José no me dijo nada acerca de su viaje a México; fue María quien me lo dijo.

Los niños hicieron sus lecciones.

Los Adams fueron a Europa.

Yo le pedí dinero a mi padre, pero no me lo dio.

Yo nunca oí esa música hasta ahora.

Ella vio la carta sobre la mesa, pero no la leyó.

Estuve tan ocupado todo el día que no tuve tiempo para almorzar.

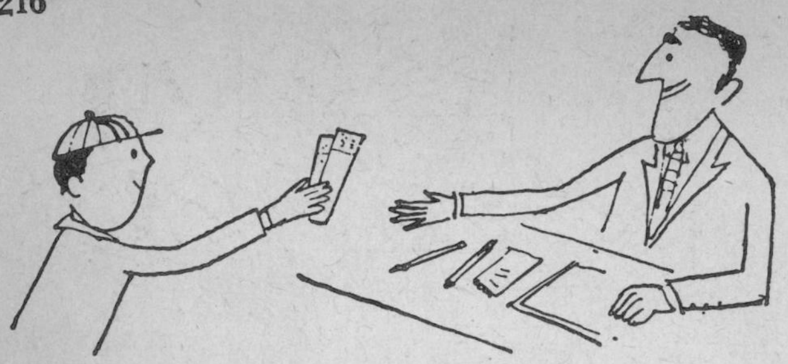

Traje los billetes; aquí los
tiene usted, señor Juárez.

Ellos no vinieron por tren; vinieron por avión.

Los niños se sintieron enfermos de repente
y no pudieron ir a la escuela.

Ellos no pudieron venir debido al mal tiempo.
María tampoco pudo venir por la misma razón.

Botones, ¿dónde puso usted mi maleta?

La puse en su habitación, caballero.

¿Fueron los niños al cine, Elena?

No, están en su habitación; no quisieron ir al cine.

¿Estuvo usted alguna vez en España?
¿Quién le dijo a usted eso?
¿Quién le dio a usted ese libro?
¿Trajo usted los libros?
¿Cuándo supo usted de su hermano?
¿Por qué no quiso ir con ella?
¿Leyó usted los periódicos?
¿Dónde pusieron los sombreros?
¿Por qué no compró usted las camisas?
¿Le gustó la película?

No, nunca estuve en España.
José me lo dijo.
El profesor me lo dio.
No, los dejé en casa.
Supe de él la semana pasada.
Yo quise ir, pero no pude.
Sí, los leí esta mañana.
Los pusieron en el otro cuarto.
Porque no me gustaron.
Sí, me encantó.

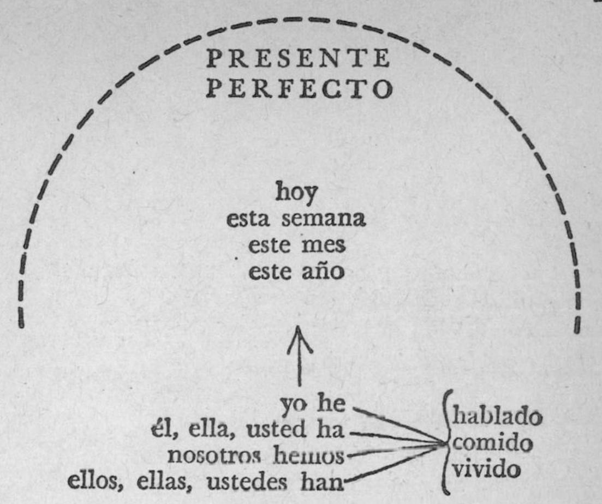

¿Con quién ha hablado usted hoy?
Yo no he hablado con nadie.
¿Quién ha dicho eso?
Yo no sé quién lo ha dicho.
¿Ha comido usted en casa esta semana?
No, esta semana no he comido en casa; he estado fuera.
¿Han estado ustedes en España este año?
No, desafortunadamente no hemos estado ni en España ni en ninguna parte.
María, ¿ha tenido tiempo de terminar el trabajo?
No, desafortunadamente no he tenido tiempo para nada.

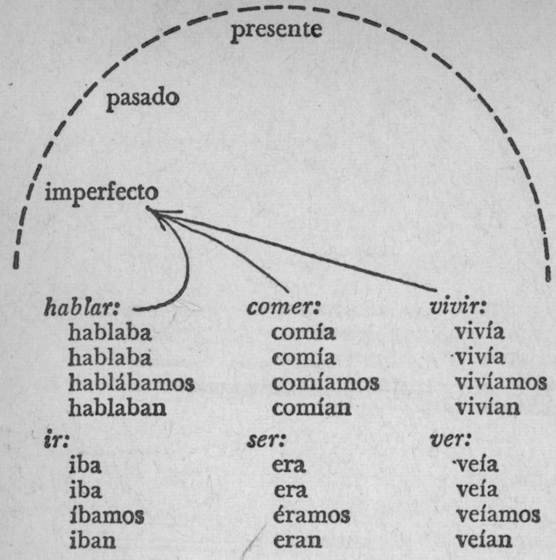

hablar:	*comer:*	*vivir:*
hablaba	comía	vivía
hablaba	comía	vivía
hablábamos	comíamos	vivíamos
hablaban	comían	vivían
ir:	*ser:*	*ver:*
iba	era	veía
iba	era	veía
íbamos	éramos	veíamos
iban	eran	veían

Ustedes hablaban español cuando yo entré.
¿A dónde iba usted tan de prisa esta mañana?
Iba de compras cuando usted me vio.
¿Qué hora era cuando usted llegó a casa?
Eran las 5:30 cuando llegué.
Yo solía ir mucho al teatro, pero ahora no voy.
María creía que yo estaba enfermo.
Nosotros no sabíamos que ellos estaban en España.
Los museos se abrían a las 9:00, pero ahora se abren a las 10:00.
Yo no sabía que los Adams eran norteamericanos.
Yo hablaba con mi mujer cuando usted entró.
(o, Yo estaba hablando con mi mujer cuando usted entró.)
Nosotros comíamos cuando ellos llegaron.
(o, Nosotros estábamos comiendo cuando ellos llegaron.)
¿Había mucho público en el teatro?
Sí, había mucho.
Cuando le llamé por teléfono anoche, usted ya se había acostado.
Acababa de leer este libro cuando usted entró.

Cuando yo era niño vivía con mis padres y hermanos. Nosotros éramos seis

hermanos: tres hermanos y tres hermanas. En ese tiempo vivíamos en San Sebastián.

La casa de mis padres daba al Mar Cantábrico. La vista era maravillosa.

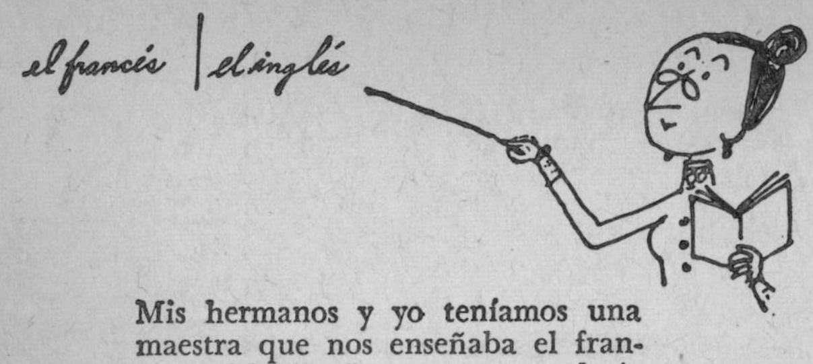

Mis hermanos y yo teníamos una maestra que nos enseñaba el francés y el inglés. La maestra nos decía

que teníamos que estudiar mucho si queríamos aprender bien el francés y el inglés. Mis hermanos los sabían mejor que yo. A mí no me gustaba estudiar.

Cuando nos levantábamos, la primera cosa que hacíamos era lavarnos. Después tomábamos el desayuno. Más tarde nos poníamos a estudiar.

No aprendíamos mucho, pero nuestro padre no nos decía nada. Él era un hombre muy bondadoso y nos quería mucho. La maestra nos tenía también gran cariño.

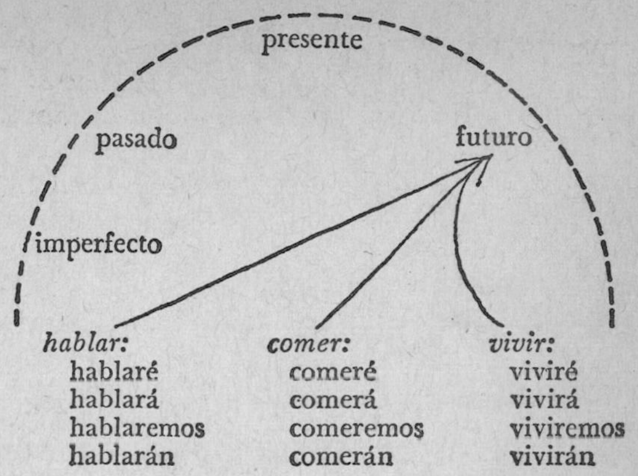

Yo hablaré mañana en español con mi profesor.
Mañana por la noche comeremos con nuestros amigos.
Nosotros pasaremos tres semanas en el Perú.
Ellos volverán el mes que viene.
Más tarde compraré todas las cosas que necesito para el viaje.
¿Dónde estarán ustedes mañana?
Le escribiré a usted desde España.
Guillermo irá a Colombia en septiembre.
¿Qué día llegará usted a Barcelona?
Trataremos de llegar a tiempo.
Ellos vendrán más tarde.
Si voy, se lo diré a usted mañana.
Yo haré lo posible por ver a usted mañana.
La veré mañana sin falta.

¿Dónde habré puesto yo mi sombrero?
Lo habrá puesto en el otro cuarto.

No veo a mi mujer por ninguna parte.
¿Dónde estará?
Estará en la cocina preparando la cena.

¿De quién será este paraguas?
Será de la señora que acaba de salir.

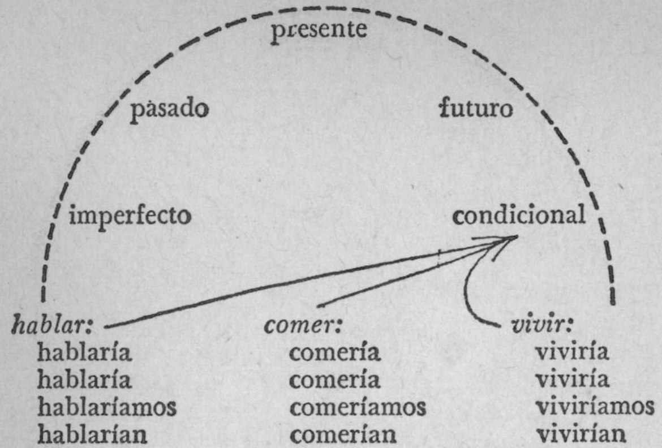

Guillermo dijo que hablaría en español con su profesor.
Le dije a José que le prestaría el dinero.
Ellos nos dijeron que irían en automóvil.
Dijimos a los niños que les compraríamos muchos regalos.
Me gustaría hablar bien el español.
Ellos preferirían quedarse en casa esta noche.
Nos llamó por teléfono para decirnos que llegaría tarde.
¿Podría usted venir mañana?
Ustedes deberían ir allá en seguida.
Me alegraría ir con ustedes, pero no puedo en este momento.
Desearían venir temprano, pero todavía no saben si podrán.
Me gustaría mucho conocerla.

¿Qué hora sería cuando ella llegó.
Serían las tres de la tarde.

¿Cuántos años tendría ella cuando se casó con Miguel?
Tendría veinticinco años.

¿Dónde pondría yo mi sombrero?
Lo pondría en la alcoba.

Habría unas cincuenta personas en la sala.
Yo creí que usted habría ido también.
No contestó porque seguramente estaría comiendo.

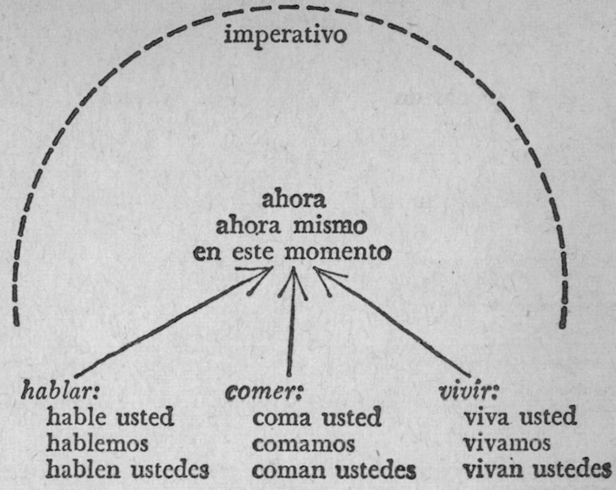

Hable usted más despacio, por favor.
Hablemos en español.
Hablen ustedes con el señor Adams acerca de ese asunto.
Lea usted esto en voz alta.
Escriba usted aquí su nombre y su dirección.
Estudien ustedes esta lección.
Aprendan ustedes estas palabras de memoria.
Espere usted en la otra habitación.
Compren ustedes hoy la ropa que necesitan.
Lleve usted estos libros al otro cuarto.
Abramos las ventanas. Hace mucho calor.
Escuchen ustedes al profesor.
No me lleve usted a ese hotel; lléveme al hotel Ritz.

cerrar:
cierre usted
cerremos
cierren ustedes

estar:
esté usted
estemos
estén ustedes

perder:
pierda usted
perdamos
pierdan ustedes

ser:
sea usted
seamos
sean ustedes

contar:
cuente usted
contemos
cuenten ustedes

hacer:
haga usted
hagamos
hagan ustedes

poner:
ponga usted
pongamos
pongan ustedes

tener:
tenga usted
tengamos
tengan ustedes

dar:
dé usted
demos
den ustedes

ir:
vaya usted
vayamos
vayan ustedes

reír:
ría usted
riamos
rían ustedes

traer:
traiga usted
traigamos
traigan ustedes

decir:
diga usted
digamos
digan ustedes

oír:
oiga usted
oigamos
oigan ustedes

saber:
sepa usted
sepamos
sepan ustedes

venir:
venga usted
vengamos
vengan ustedes

encender:
encienda usted
encendamos
enciendan ustedes

pedir:
pida usted
pidamos
pidan ustedes

salir:
salga usted
salgamos
salgan ustedes

volver:
vuelva usted
volvamos
vuelvan ustedes

No cierren ustedes las ventanas; no las cierren.

Cierren ustedes los libros; ciérrenlos.

Cuente usted las personas que hay en la sala; cuéntelas.

No cuente usted los asientos; no los cuente.

Deme usted el dinero. No se lo dé a mi mujer, démelo a mí.

Juanito, dele las gracias a la señora. No me las dé a mí, déselas a la señora.

Dígame usted lo que hizo anoche. Dígamelo ahora, no me lo diga más tarde.

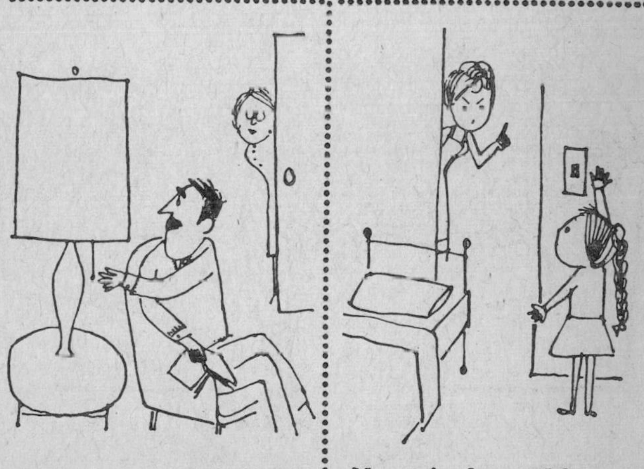

Encienda usted las luces de la sala; enciéndalas.

No encienda usted las luces de la alcoba; no las encienda.

Esté usted aquí a las 9:00 en punto.

Haga usted las cosas bien. Hágalas bien, no las haga mal.

Vayan ustedes a mi casa; no vayan a casa de María.

Váyase usted ahora mismo.

No se vaya todavía.

Oiga usted bien lo que le digo; oígalo bien.

Pídale usted los libros al profesor; no me los pida a mí.

No pierda usted la dirección y el número de teléfono de José; no los pierda.

Pongan ustedes los sombreros
en la silla.
No los pongan en la cama,
pónganlos en la silla.

No se ría usted de lo que le digo; hablo en serio.

No salgan ustedes tan tarde;
salgan más temprano.

¡No sean ustedes malos, niños; sean buenos!

Tenga usted cuidado al cruzar la calle.

¡Guillermo; venga usted acá!

Vuelva usted mañana a la misma hora.

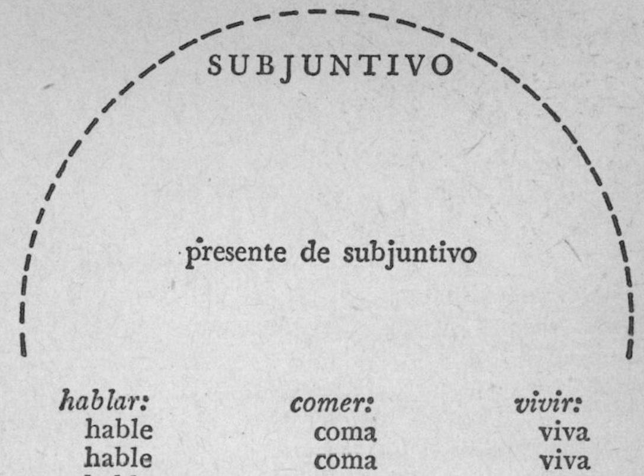

SUBJUNTIVO

presente de subjuntivo

hablar:	*comer:*	*vivir:*
hable	coma	viva
hable	coma	viva
hablemos	comamos	vivamos
hablen	coman	vivan

Ellos quieren que usted cierre la ventana.
Yo no quiero que ustedes digan nada a nadie.
Ella desea que nosotros estemos aquí temprano.
Mis padres no desean que yo vaya sola.
Dígales usted que esperen aquí.
Mi padre insiste en que yo estudie para médico.
Ellos prefieren que usted salga hoy.
¿Por qué temen ellos que usted no vuelva?
Yo temo que ella se ponga enferma.
Sentimos que ustedes no puedan venir.
Mi amigo duda que yo haga el trabajo bien.
¿Cree usted que vengan ellos hoy?
Yo no creo que ellos puedan venir hoy.
Me extraña mucho que él diga eso.
Me sorprende que usted no conozca al señor.
Es necesario que usted vaya ahora mismo.

Ellos no quieren venir.
Yo quiero ir esta noche.
Ella no duda de que ustedes irán.
María cree que es muy tarde.
Es necesario ir ahora mismo.

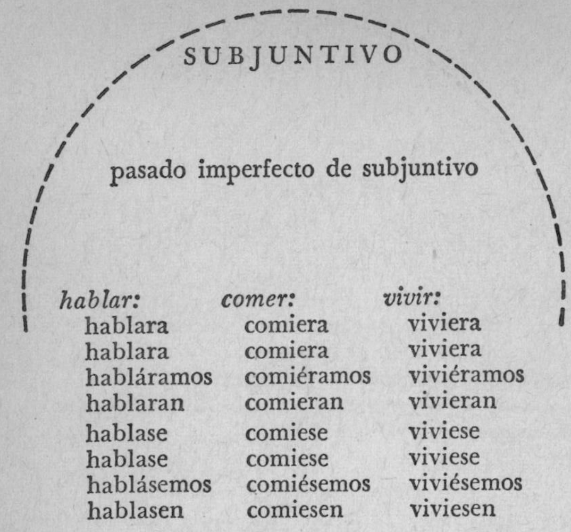

SUBJUNTIVO

pasado imperfecto de subjuntivo

hablar:	*comer:*	*vivir:*
hablara	comiera	viviera
hablara	comiera	viviera
habláramos	comiéramos	viviéramos
hablaran	comieran	vivieran
hablase	comiese	viviese
hablase	comiese	viviese
hablásemos	comiésemos	viviésemos
hablasen	comiesen	viviesen

Ellos querían que usted cerrara la ventana.
Yo no quería que ustedes dijeran nada a nadie.
Ella deseaba que nosotros estuviéramos aquí temprano.
Mis padres no deseaban que yo fuera sola.
Les dije a ustedes que esperaran aquí.
Mi padre insistió en que yo estudiara para médico.
Ellos preferían que usted saliera hoy.
¿Por qué temían ellos que usted no volviera?
Yo temí que ella se pusiera enferma.
Sentimos que ustedes no pudiesen venir.
Mi amigo dudó que yo hiciera el trabajo bien.
¿Creyó usted que ellos vinieran hoy?
Yo no creía que ellos pudieran venir hoy.
Me extrañó mucho que él dijera eso.
Me sorprendió que usted no conociera al señor.
Era necesario que ustedes fueran hoy mismo.

Ellos no quisieron venir.
Yo quería ir esta noche.
Ella no dudó que ustedes fueron.
María creyó que era muy tarde.
Fue necesario ir allá.

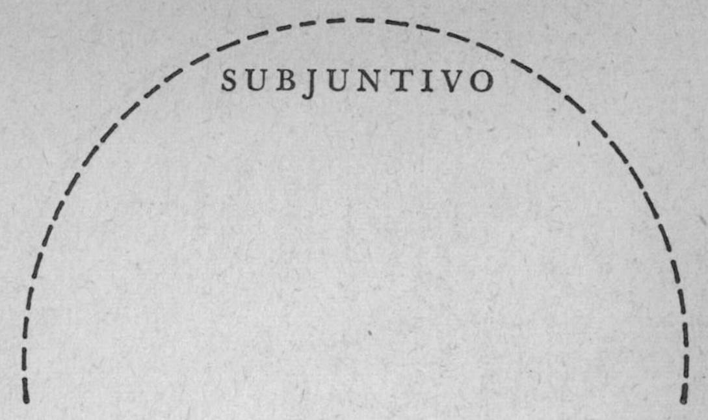

SUBJUNTIVO

Busco un hombre que hable español.
Yo no conocía a nadie que hablara inglés.
Iremos a menos que haga mal tiempo.
Tenemos que salir antes que él venga.
Telefonearé a usted tan pronto como sepa
el día en que salimos.
Dígale usted a María que venga acá.
Yo no saldré hasta que usted vuelva.
Si tuviera dinero, iría a Sud América.
No tengo tiempo; pero si lo tuviera,
estudiaría lenguas.
María no está en Nueva York; pero si estuviera,
la invitaría a comer.
Yo no tengo dinero; pero si lo tuviera,
compraría una casa en el campo.

Busco al hombre que habla español.
Si tengo tiempo, vendré mañana.
Si Elena viene, la invitaré.

Adiós amigos.
Que apprendan mucho!

Grammar

The Articles

DEFINITE ARTICLES

el is used before a masculine singular noun: *el hombre,* the man.

la is used before a feminine singular noun: *la mujer,* the woman.

los is used before a masculine plural noun: *los hombres,* the men.

las is used before a feminine plural noun: *las mujeres,* the women.

lo is used before masculine forms of adjectives, and past participles used as nouns: *lo mismo,* the same; *lo contrario,* the opposite; *lo escrito,* the (that which is) written.

The definite articles are generally used in Spanish whenever they are used in English, except that in Spanish they are repeated before each noun to which they refer: *el hombre y la mujer,* the man and (the) woman. They also appear:

1. before nouns, including infinitives, used in a general sense: *El pan es bueno.* (Bread is good.) *El viajar es agradable.* (Traveling is pleasant.)

2. before titles (except *don,* and direct address): *El señor López está aquí.* (Mr. Lopez is here.) But: *Buenos días, señor López.* (Good morning, Mr.

Lopez.) *Don Alfonso está aquí.* (*Don* Alfonso is here.)

3. before days of the week (except after *ser*) and seasons: *Voy el lunes.* (I am going Monday.) But: *Hoy es lunes.* (Today is Monday.)

4. before names of languages, except immediately after *hablar*, to speak; *de*, of; *en*, in: *Estudio el español.* (I study Spanish.) But: *Hablo español.* (I speak Spanish.)

5. before names of certain cities and countries, and with modified geographical names: *el Perú*, Peru; *la Argentina*, Argentina; *la América del Norte*, North America.

6. before parts of the body and articles of clothing, instead of possessive adjectives: *Me lavo las manos.* (I wash my hands.) *Me pongo el sombrero.* (I put on my hat.)

7. before terms of time and quantity, instead of "a," "an," and "per": *un dólar la docena*, a dollar a dozen.

The definite article *el* forms contractions with the prepositions *a* and *de: a* and *el* become *al* (to the, at the) and *de* and *el* become *del* (of the, about the, from the). These contractions are used only before masculine singular nouns: *Doy el libro al hombre.* (I'm giving the book to the man.) *Hablamos del libro.* (We're talking about the book.)

INDEFINITE ARTICLES

un is used before a masculine singular noun: *un hombre*, a (one) man.

una is used before a feminine singular noun: *una mujer*, a (one) woman.

The indefinite articles are generally used in Spanish whenever they are used in English, except that in

Spanish they are repeated before each noun to which they refer: *un hombre y una mujer,* a man and (a) woman.

They are omitted:

1. before unmodified predicate nouns denoting profession, occupation, nationality, and rank: *El es médico.* (He is a doctor.) *Ella es mexicana.* (She is Mexican.) But: *El es un médico famoso.* (He is a famous doctor.) *Ella es una mexicana simpática.* (She is a charming Mexican.)

2. before *otro, otra,* another; *cierto, cierta,* a certain; *cien, ciento,* a hundred; *mil,* a thousand; and *otro hombre,* another man.

3. after *qué,* what a: *¡Qué mujer!* (What a woman!) *¡Qué día!* (What a day!)

4. when the numerical "one" is superfluous: *No lleva sombrero.* (He doesn't wear a hat.)

Note that when *un* or *una* appear in the plural (*unos, unas*), they mean "some."

Nouns

The gender of nouns is either masculine or feminine.

1. Nouns ending in *-o,* are masculine: *el muchacho,* the boy; *el libro,* the book. A common exception is *la mano,* the hand. Most nouns ending in *l, r,* and *s* are also masculine: *el papel,* the paper; *el placer,* the pleasure; *el mes,* the month. Common exceptions are: *la sal,* the salt; *la flor,* the flower; and *la tos,* the cough.

2. Nouns ending in *-a* are feminine: *la muchacha,* the girl; *la casa,* the house. Common exceptions are: *el día,* the day; *el sofá,* the sofa; *el mapa,* the map; *el drama,* the drama; and *el planeta,* the planet. Most

nouns ending in *d, -ión, -umbre,* and *z* are also feminine: *la ciudad,* the city; *la atención,* the attention; *la costumbre,* the custom; *la paz,* the peace. Common exceptions are: *el arroz,* the rice; and *el lápiz,* the pencil.

3. Other endings are either masculine or feminine: *el corazón,* the heart; *la razón,* the reason, the cause.

4. Nouns denoting male beings are masculine, and nouns denoting female beings are feminine, regardless of endings: *el hombre,* the man; *la mujer,* the woman; *el artista,* the (man) artist; *la artista,* the (woman) artist.

In Spanish, infinitives, not present participles, are used with the article *el,* as nouns: *El viajar es agradable.* (Traveling is pleasant.) Nouns are used, not as adjectives but as nouns, with *de: un reloj de oro,* a gold watch. Adjectives with definite articles are used as nouns: *el blanco,* the white one; *la blanca,* the white one; *el grande y el pequeño,* the big one and the small one.

The number of nouns is either singular or plural.

5. To make nouns plural when the singular ends in a vowel, add *s: los muchachos,* the boys; *las muchachas,* the girls; *los hombres,* the men.

6. To form the plural when the singular ends in a consonant other than *s,* add *-es: las mujeres,* the women; *las ciudades,* the cities.

7. To form the plural when the singular ends in *z,* change the *z* to *c* and add *-es: la paz* (peace), *las paces; el lápiz* (pencil), *los lápices.*

8. Nouns of more than one syllable ending in *-es* or *-is* do not change in the plural: *el lunes* (Monday), *los lunes; la crisis* (crisis), *las crisis.* But: *el mes* (month), *los meses.*

9. Plural masculine nouns may include both genders: *los padres* (*el padre y la madre*), the parents (father and mother); *los muchachos,* the boys, the boy and the girl, or the boys and the girls.

10. Use the singular noun instead of the plural to identify an object (a part of a person's body or an article of clothing), one of which is possessed by each member of a group. In such cases the definite article is used instead of the possessive adjective (see Definite Articles, 6, above).

11. If, however, the object is plural, use the plural: *Los niños se lavaron la cara* (one each) *y las manos* (two each). (The children washed their faces and their hands.) *Nosotros nos pusimos el sombrero* (one each) *y los guantes* (two each). (We put on our hats and gloves.)

Adjectives

The gender of adjectives is either masculine or feminine.

1. Adjectives ending in *-o* in the masculine singular change the *-o* to *-a* to form the feminine: *blanco, blanca,* white.

2. Adjectives of nationality ending in a consonant in the masculine singular add *-a* to form the feminine: *español, española,* Spanish; *inglés, inglesa,* English; *alemán, alemana,* German.

3. Most other adjectives have the same form in both genders: *verde,* green; *fácil,* easy; *cortés,* polite; *feliz,* happy; *mejor,* better; *peor,* worse. There is an exception to this rule: Adjectives ending in *-ón, -án,*

-or (but not comparatives ending in *-or*) add *-a* to form the feminine: *hablador, habladora,* talkative; *juguetón, juguetona,* playful; *holgazán, holgazana,* lazy.

The number of adjectives is either singular or plural.

4. To make adjectives plural when the singular ends in a vowel, add *-s: blanco, blancos; blanca, blancas,* white; *verde, verdes,* green; *española, españolas,* Spanish.

5. To form the plural when the singular ends in a consonant, add *-es* (change *z* to *c* and add *-es*): *fácil, fáciles,* easy; *cortés, corteses,* polite; *feliz, felices,* happy; *español, españoles,* Spanish.

6. An adjective modifying two or more singular or plural nouns of different genders is in the masculine plural: *el hombre y la mujer altos,* the tall man and woman.

Adjectives agree in gender and number with the noun or pronoun they modify (see 6, above): *la casa blanca,* the white house; *el hombre alto,* the tall man; *los edificios altos,* the tall buildings.

POSITION OF ADJECTIVES

1. When an adjective distinguishes a noun (person or thing) from others of its class, it is called a descriptive adjective. This kind of adjective is placed after the noun: *el hombre alto,* the tall man; *un muchacho pobre,* a poor boy; *una muchacha bonita,* a pretty girl.

2. Some descriptive adjectives are placed before the noun to denote an inherent or logical quality in the person or thing: *¡pobre muchacho!,* poor boy; *la blanca nieve,* the white snow.

3. When an adjective does not describe a noun, it is called a limiting adjective. This kind of adjective is placed before the noun: *dos casas,* two houses; *mi libro,* my book; *este hombre,* this man.

Before a masculine singular noun, the adjectives *bueno* (good), *malo* (bad), *alguno* (some), *ninguno* (no one), *uno* (one), *primero* (first), and *tercero* (third), drop the ending *-o: el primer día,* the first day; *un buen muchacho,* a good boy. The adjective *grande* (big, large) can drop its *-de,* but then it means "great": *un gran hombre,* a great man; *una gran mujer,* a great woman. *Cicnto* (a hundred) drops its *-to* before a noun: *cien hombres,* a hundred men; *cien mujeres,* a hundred women.

Past participles used as adjectives agree in gender and number with the nouns they modify: *el mes pasado,* last month; *la semana pasada,* last week.

Possessives

ADJECTIVES

Masculine	Feminine	
mi	*mi*	my
mis	*mis*	my
su	*su*	your, his, her, its
sus	*sus*	your, his, her, its
nuestro	*nuestra*	our
nuestros	*nuestras*	our
su	*su*	your, their
sus	*sus*	your, their

PRONOUNS

Masculine	Feminine	
mío	*mía*	mine
míos	*mías*	mine
suyo	*suya*	yours, his, hers
suyos	*suyas*	yours, his, hers
nuestro	*nuestra*	ours
nuestros	*nuestras*	ours
suyo	*suya*	yours, theirs
suyos	*suyas*	yours, theirs

1. Possessives agree in gender and number with the thing or things possessed, not with the possessor: *mi casa,* my house; *mis casas,* my houses; *nuestro libro,* our book; *nuestra casa,* our house.

2. *Su casa* means: your house, his house, her house, its house, their house. For clarification, instead of *su, sus,* use *de usted, de él, de ella, de ustedes, de ellos, de ellas: la casa de usted,* your house; *la casa de ella,* her house.

3. Use the definite (or indefinite) article instead of a possessive adjective when referring to a part of a person's body or an article of clothing (see Definite Articles, 6, and Nouns, 10, above): *Ella se lava las manos.* (She washes her hands.) *Yo me quito el sombrero.* (I take off my hat.)

4. The possessive pronouns agree in gender and number with the thing or things they replace—that is, with the thing or things possessed, not with the possessor. Use *el, la, los,* or *las* before the pronouns: *Su casa es grande, la mía es pequeña.* (Your house is big, mine is small.) *Mis amigos hablan inglés, los suyos*

hablan español. (My friends speak English, yours speak Spanish.)

5. *Suyo* means: yours, his, hers, theirs. For clarification, instead of *suyo* (*suya, suyos, suyas*), use *el* (*la, los, las*) *de usted, de él, de ella, de ustedes, de ellos, de ellas: Mi casa es grande, la de ellos es pequeña.* (My house is big, theirs is small.) *Los amigos de usted hablan inglés, los de ella hablan español.* (Your friends speak English, hers speak Spanish.)

6. Omit *el, la, los,* and *las* when a form of *ser* (to be) is used before possessives: *La casa es mía.* (The house is mine.) *Los libros son míos, las plumas son de ustedes.* (The books are mine, the pens are yours.)

7. The English possessives "-'," " 's," and "s' " are translated by *el* (*la, los, las*) *de: Mi casa y la de María.* (My house and Mary's.) *La casa de María y la del profesor.* (Mary's house and the professor's.) *El libro de los muchachos y el de los profesores.* (The boys' book and the professors'.)

8. The English "of" drops out before the possessive pronouns: *un amigo mío,* a friend of mine.

Demonstratives

ADJECTIVES

Masculine	Feminine	
este	*esta*	this (near the speaker)
estos	*estas*	these
ese	*esa*	that (near the person spoken to)
esos	*esas*	those

aquel	*aquella*	that (away from both)
aquellos	*aquellas*	those

PRONOUNS

Masculine	Feminine	Neuter	
éste	*ésta*	*esto*	this (near the speaker)
éstos	*éstas*		these
ése	*ésa*	*eso*	that (near the person spoken to)
ésos	*ésas*		those
aquél	*aquélla*	*aquello*	that (away from both)
aquéllos	*aquéllas*		those

1. These adjectives agree in gender and number with the nouns they modify: *este hombre,* this man; *esta mujer,* this woman; *estos hombres,* these men; *estas mujeres,* these women.

2. These pronouns agree in gender and number with the nouns they replace. They have a written accent on the stressed syllable to distinguish them from the adjectives: *Esta casa y ésa son mías.* (This house and that one are mine.) *Esa casa y aquélla son de María.* (That house and that one over there are Mary's.) *Estos libros y ésos son del profesor.* (These books and those are the professor's.)

3. The neuter pronouns are used when they do not have a specific noun for an antecedent: *¿Qué es esto?* (What is this?) *¿Qué es eso?* (What is that?)

4. Demonstrative pronouns are often replaced by *el de, la de, los de, las de* (that of, those of, the one of,

the one with, those with, the one in, those in): *mi casa y la de mi amigo,* my house and that of my friend (my friend's). *La del vestido azul es mi hermana.* (The one in the blue dress is my sister.)

5. Demonstrative pronouns are often replaced by *el que, la que, los que, las que* and a verb (the one that, those that, the one which, those which, the one who, those who): *El hombre que habla español es español, el que habla ingles es norteamericano.* (The man who speaks Spanish is a Spaniard, the one who speaks English is an American.)

Pronouns

PERSONAL PRONOUNS

		Indirect object		Direct object	
yo	I	*me*	to me	*me*	me
usted	you	*le*	to you	*le* or *lo, la*	you
él	he	*le*	to him	*le* or *lo*	him
ella	she	*le*	to her	*la*	her
nosotros	we	*nos*	to us	*nos*	us
nosotras	we	*nos*	to us	*nos*	us
ustedes	you	*les*	to you	*los, las*	you
ellos	they	*les*	to them	*los*	them
ellas	they	*les*	to them	*las*	them
		le	to it	*lo, la*	it

With preposition		Reflexive	
mí	me	*me*	myself
usted	you	*se*	yourself

él	him	*se*	himself
ella	her	*se*	herself
nosotros	us	*nos*	ourselves
nosotras	us	*nos*	ourselves
ustedes	you	*se*	yourselves
ellos	them	*se*	themselves
ellas	them	*se*	themselves
él, ella, ello	it	*se*	itself

Note that except for the first person singular, subject and prepositional pronouns are identical.

1. Subject pronouns, except *usted* and *ustedes,* are usually omitted. Do not omit them in a compound subject or in answering a question where the interrogative pronoun *quién* or *quiénes* (or any other pronoun) may require *yo, usted,* etc., for an answer: *Usted y yo hablamos español.* (You and I speak Spanish.) *¿Quién habla español aquí? Yo hablo español.* (Who speaks Spanish here? I speak Spanish.) Do not omit them in a contrasting statement, but note that when the contrast requires a preposition it is the prepositional pronouns that are used, not the subject pronouns: *Ella habla inglés, pero yo no.* (She speaks English, but not I.) *Usted no estudia con él, estudia conmigo.* (You are not studying with him, you are studying with me.) Observe that an indirect or direct object pronoun is never the object of a preposition: *Hablé con él* (not *con le*). (I spoke with him.)

POSITION OF PRONOUNS

1. Subject + indirect object + direct object + verb, + prepositional (if needed): *Usted me lo dijo a mí*

(*a mí* for emphasis). (You told it to me.) *Usted no me lo dijo a mí, se lo dijo a ella* (*a mí* and *a ella* for contrast and clearness). (You did not tell it to me, you told it to her.)

2. Place indirect and direct object pronouns before verbs, but attach them—in that same order—after infinitives, present participles, and affirmative commands: *Usted me lo dice* (present tense). (You are telling it to me.) *Usted me lo decía* (imperfect). (You were telling it to me.) *Usted me lo dijo* (preterite). (You told it to me.) *Usted me lo dirá* (future). (You will tell it to me.) *Usted me lo diría* (conditional). (You would tell it to me.) *Dudo que usted me lo diga* (present subjunctive). (I doubt you will tell it to me.) *Dudé que me lo dijera* (imperfect subjunctive). (I doubted you told it to me.) *No me lo diga usted* (negative command). (Don't tell it to me.) But: *Usted quiere decírmelo* (infinitive). (You wish to tell it to me.) *Usted está diciéndomelo* (present participle). (You are telling it to me.) *Dígamelo usted* (affirmative command). (Tell it to me.) When an infinitive or a present participle is preceded by a main verb, however, the pronouns may appear before the main verb: *Usted me lo quiere decir. Usted me lo está diciendo.*

Incidentally, the neuter direct object pronoun *lo* is often used to refer to an idea or to a whole statement: *José salió ayer. Lo sabe usted? Sí, lo sé.* (Joseph left yesterday. Do you know that? Yes, I know it.) *María es una mujer encantadora. Lo sé.* (Mary is a charming woman. I know it.) *Lo* may also refer to a masculine or feminine adjective in a preceding statement: *¿Son ustedes norteamericanos? Sí, lo somos.* (Are you Americans? Yes, we are.)

3. When the indirect object pronouns *le* and *les* are followed by the direct object pronouns *lo, la, los*

or *las,* change *le* or *les* to *se* for better sound: *El se los da a usted* (not *él le los*). (He gives them to you.) *Yo se la doy a ustedes* (not *yo les la*). (I give it to you.)

4. *Le* and *les* by themselves, like *su, sus,* and *suyo, suyos,* are not explicit enough in meaning. Although in conversation we usually know for whom these pronouns stand, for clarity use: *a usted, a el, a ella, a ustedes, a ellos, a ellas, al señor, a la señora, a María, a José,* etc., after the verb when *le* and *les* seem vague.

PREPOSITIONAL PRONOUNS

1. Except for *mí,* use subject pronouns as objects of prepositions: *El libro es para mí.* (The book is for me.) *La carta es para usted* (*para él, para ella, para nosotros, para ustedes, para ellos, para ellas*). (The letter is for you, etc.) *Ellos hablan de nosotros.* (They are speaking of us.) "With me" becomes *conmigo: Ella va conmigo.* (She is going with me.)

2. All nouns in Spanish are either masculine or feminine. When the object pronoun "it," or its plural "them," is used after a preposition, determine the gender of the noun to which "it" or "them" refers and then translate: *¿Ha visto usted mi pluma, María? Sí, escribo con ella.* (Have you seen my pen, Mary? Yes, I am writing with it.) *¿Cuánto pagó usted por los billetes? Pagué cinco dólares por ellos.* (How much did you pay for the tickets? I paid five dollars for them.) When "it" is used after a preposition to refer to an idea or statement, use *ello* in Spanish: *Hablábamos de ello cuando usted entró.* (We were talking about it when you came in.)

REFLEXIVE PRONOUNS

1. Use reflexive pronouns when the action of a verb refers back to the subject: *Yo me levanto tem-*

prano. (I get up early.) *Usted se acuesta tarde.* (You go to bed late.) *Usted se lava la cara* (see Definite Articles, 6, above). (You are washing your face.) *María se lava las manos.* (Mary is washing her hands.)

The position of reflexive pronouns is the same as that of object pronouns, but the *s* of the first person plural is dropped in the affirmative command before adding the reflexive pronoun *nos: Lavémonos antes de comer.* (Let us wash before eating.) But: *No nos lavemos antes de comer.* (Let us not wash before eating.)

2. Instead of a passive construction when the agent is not expressed, use a reflexive construction with *se* or the third person plural of the verb (see *Ser* and *Estar*, below): *Aquí se habla español,* or *Aquí hablan español.* (Spanish is spoken here.) *Se dice que ellos vendrán mañana,* or *Dicen que ellos vendrán mañana.* (It is said that they will come tomorrow.) *Se prohibe fumar,* or *Prohiben fumar.* (No smoking.)

RELATIVE PRONOUNS

1. *Que* (who, whom, that, which) may be the subject or object of a verb. A relative pronoun in Spanish is never left out. It may refer to persons, or things: *No conozco al hombre que viene esta noche.* (I don't know the gentleman who is coming tonight.) *Hablé con el abogado que usted me recomendó.* (I spoke with the lawyer whom you recommended to me.) *Esta es la corbata que compré.* (This is the necktie that I bought.) *El sombrero que está sobre la silla es mío.* (The hat which is on the chair is mine.)

2. After a preposition, *que* refers only to things: *La casa en que viven mis padres es nueva.* (The house in which my parents live is new.) *La pluma con que usted escribe no es buena.* (The pen with which you

are writing is no good.)

3. *Quien* (and its plural *quienes*) always agrees in number with its antecedent. It refers only to a person and, as a relative pronoun, it is used mostly after a preposition: *El señor de quien usted habla es médico.* (The gentleman of whom you are speaking is a doctor.) *Los hombres con quienes ustedes van hablan muy bien el español.* (The men with whom you are going speak Spanish very well.) When "who" or "whom" is used after some part of "to be," following a noun or pronoun, translate as *quien* or *quienes* (not *que*): *Soy yo quien lo hizo.* (It is I who did it.)

4. *El cual* (*la cual, los cuales, las cuales*) may be used instead of *que* or *quien* (see *el que,* etc. under Demonstratives, 5, above): *Vi al hermano de María, el cual llegó ayer del Perú* (*el cual* clearly refers to *el hermano* rather than to *María*). (I saw Mary's brother, who arrived yesterday from Peru.)

5. *Lo que* refers to no definite noun, but to a whole idea, and may be translated by "which," "that which," "what," or "whatever": *No entiendo lo que usted dice.* (I don't understand what you are saying.) *Lo que usted diga está bien.* (Whatever you say is all right.) *No ha llegado todavía, lo que me sorprende mucho.* (He has not arrived yet, which surprises me very much.)

6. *Cuyo* (*cuya, cuyos, cuyas*) means "whose," but, in questions, "whose" is translated by *de quién* or *de quiénes: ¿De quién es este sombrero?* (Whose hat is this?) But: *Preferimos las tiendas cuyos precios son módicos.* (We prefer the stores whose prices are moderate.)

INTERROGATIVE PRONOUNS

1. *Qué* (what, which) asks for a definition or in-

quires about an unnamed thing or idea: *¿Qué es Buenos Aires?* (What is Buenos Aires?) *¿En qué calle vive usted?* (In what street do you live?) *¿De qué hablan ustedes?* (What are you talking about?) *¿De qué mujer hablan ustedes?* (What woman are you talking about?) *¿Qué tiene usted en la mano?* (What do you have in your hand?)

2. *Cuál* (*cuáles*) means "which," "which one" (which ones), or "what." Use *cuál* before the verb *ser* when the answer can be short—a number, a name, etc.: *¿Cuál es el precio?* (What is the price?) *¿Cuáles son sus libros?* (Which are your books?) *¿Con cuál de sus amigos va usted a México?* (With which one of your friends are you going to Mexico?)

3. *Quién* (*quiénes*) means "who," or "whom": *¿Quién pregunta por mí?* (Who is asking for me?) *¿A quién escribe usted?* (To whom are you writing?) *¿De quién es este libro?* (Whose book is this?)

Adverbs

1. Use adverbs with verbs to describe how, where, or when an action takes place. An adverb may be placed in different parts of a sentence, but when in doubt, place it right after the verb: *Yo no vivo lejos, vivo cerca.* (I don't live far away, I live nearby.) *Si no podemos ir ahora, iremos después.* (If we cannot go now, we shall go later.) *Yo escribo a menudo a mis amigos.* (I write often to my friends.)

2. Form adverbs from feminine forms of adjectives by adding *-mente: reciente* (recent), *recientemente* (recently); *principal* (main), *principalmente* (mainly); *feliz* (happy, fortunate), *felizmente* (happily, fortu-

nately). Adjectives ending in *-o* change *-o* to *-a* before adding *-mente: perfecto* (perfect), *perfectamente* (perfectly).

3. When such adverbs are used in a series add *-mente* to the last one and keep the others in the feminine form: *Usted habla clara y distintamente.* (You speak clearly and distinctly.)

Comparatives and Superlatives

1. The comparative with adjectives (and adverbs) is made with *más* (*menos*) + the adjective: *más* (*menos*) *alto* (*alta, altos, altas*), taller (less tall). The superlative is made with *el* (*la, los, las*) + *más* (*menos*) *alto* (*alta, altos, altas*): *el más alto,* the tallest.

2. "Than" + a number, whether the whole sense be affirmative or be negative, is translated as *de* + the number; but *no . . . más que* may be used with the meaning "only": *Tengo más* (*menos*) *de veinte libros.* (I have more (less) than twenty books.) But: *No tengo más que veinte libros.* (I have only twenty books.)

3. "Than" + a noun or pronoun is translated as *que* + the noun or pronoun: *Tengo más* (*menos*) *tiempo que María* (*ella*). (I have more (less) time than Mary (she).) *Ellos saben más* (*español*) *que yo.* (They know more (Spanish) than I.)

4. "Than" + a clause implying for comparison a noun not repeated from the main clause is translated as *del* (*de la, de los, de las*) *que* + the clause: *Mi mujer tiene más sombreros de los que necesita.* (My wife has more hats than (the hats that) she needs.) When the comparison is made with a whole idea in a main clause ending in an adjective or an adverb, use

de lo que: Ella sabe más de lo que usted cree. (She knows more than you think (she knows).)

5. "In" and "of" after a superlative are translated as *de: La casa blanca es la más (menos) hermosa de todas.* (The white house is the most (least) beautiful of all.)

6. The comparison of equality, with "as" or "so" + an adjective or adverb + "as" is translated by *tan* + the adjective or adverb + *como: Usted es tan alto como él.* (You are as tall as he.) *Ella habla tan bien (claramente) como usted.* (She speaks as well (clearly) as you.)

7. The comparison of equality, with "as (so) much" or "as (so) many" + a noun + "as," is translated by *tanto (tanta, tantos, tantas)* + the noun + *como: Yo no tengo tanto tiempo como usted.* (I haven't as much time as you.) *Ella sabe tantas palabras como nosotros.* (She knows as many words as we do.)

8. A verb + "as (so) much as" + a noun or pronoun is translated by the verb + *tanto como: Yo no estudio tanto como usted.* (I do not study as much as you.)

9. Four adjectives are compared irregularly:

bueno,-a–good	*buenos,-as*–good
mejor–better	*mejores*–better
el (la) mejor–the best	*los (las) mejores*–the best
malo,-a–bad	*malos,-as*–bad
peor–worse	*peores*–worse
el peor–the worst	*los peores*–the worst
grande–large	*grandes*–large
mayor–larger	*mayores*–larger
el mayor–the largest	*los mayores*–the largest

pequeño,-a—small	*pequeños,-as*—small
menor—smaller	*menores*—smaller
el menor—the smallest	*los menores*—the smallest

Note that *grande* and *pequeño* are compared both regularly and irregularly; regularly, they refer to size: *grande, más grande, el más grande;* irregularly, they refer to age or rank: *grande, mayor, el mayor,* etc.

10. Four adverbs are compared irregularly:

bien	—	well	*mejor*	—	better, best
mal	—	bad, badly	*peor*	—	worse, worst
mucho	—	much	*más*	—	more, most
poco	—	little	*menos*	—	less, least

Note that the superlative of adverbs may be formed with the neuter article *lo,* followed by a word or phrase expressing possibility: *Vino lo más pronto posible.* (He came as soon as possible.)

11. Adverbs of place: *aquí,* here; *ahí,* there; *allí,* there, over there; *acá,* here; *allá,* there, over there. *Acá* and *allá* are mostly used with motion: *Venga usted acá.* (Come here, please.)

12. The absolute superlative of adjectives (this superlative does not denote comparison) is formed either by placing *muy* before the adjective or by placing the suffix *-ísimo* (*-ísima, -ísimos, -ísimas*) after it. It is expressed in English by "very," "most," or "exceedingly" + the adjective: *muy fácil,* very easy; *muy grande,* very large; *facilísimo,* very (most, etc.) easy; *grandísimo,* very (most, etc.) large: *una lección facilísima,* an exceedingly easy lesson; *una mujer hermosísima,* a very beautiful woman. When the adjective ends in a consonant, add *-ísimo* directly to it; when it ends in a

vowel, drop the vowel and add *-ísimo*. Please note that the superlative of *mucho* (much, very much) is *muchísimo,* never *muy mucho.*

Negatives and Positives

Negatives and positives are words that fall into pairs, one with a positive meaning and its companion with a negative meaning. Among the positives are *algo,* something, anything; *alguien,* somebody, someone, anyone, anybody; *alguno* (*-a, -os, -as*), someone, anyone (some, any); *siempre,* always; *también,* also, too. Among the negatives are *nada,* nothing, not anything; *nadie,* nobody, not anybody, no one; *ninguno* (*-a, -os, -as*), nobody, no one, none, no, not . . . any; *nunca, jamás,* never, not . . . ever; *tampoco,* neither, not . . . either; *ni . . . ni,* neither . . . nor; *no . . . más, ya no . . . más,* no longer; *en mi vida,* never in my life.

To make a verb negative, place *no* or any other negative before the verb; when a negative word is used after the verb, *no* is required before the verb (double negation is very common in Spanish): *No veo nunca a María.* (I never see Mary.) *En mi vida he visto semejante cosa.* (Never in my life have I seen such a thing.) *María no habla ruso. Yo tampoco.* (Mary does not speak Russian. Neither do I.)

Conjunctions

(See Vocabulary for *y* and *o*.)

1. "But," as a conjunction, is commonly *pero* (sometimes *mas*): *Este cuarto es pequeño, pero me gusta.* (This room is small, but I like it.) *Escribo y leo el*

alemán, pero no lo hablo. (I write and read German, but I do not speak it.)

2. "But" introducing a direct contrast after a negative verb is translated by *sino* when no verb follows or when the following verb is in an infinitive: *Este cuarto no es grande, sino pequeño.* (This room is not big, but small.) *Yo no voy a Buenos Aires, sino a Lima.* (I am not going to Buenos Aires, but to Lima.) *Los niños no quieren estudiar, sino jugar.* (The children do not want to study, but to play.)

3. "But" is usually translated by *sino que* when the first verb is negative and the second is contrasting, affirmative, and not an infinitive: *Los niños no estudian, sino que juegan.* (The children are not studying, but (on the contrary) they are playing.)

Prepositions

a, con, de, para, por

A

1. Use *a* to introduce the direct object (*a* always introduces the indirect object) when the direct object is a definite person, a friendly animal, a proper geographical noun (but not when it's preceded by a definite article), a personified noun, or a pronoun referring to a person (but not when it's an object pronoun): *Yo conozco al señor Adams.* (I know Mr. Adams.) *El muchacho llama a su perro.* (The boy is calling his dog.) *Deseo visitar a España.* (I wish to visit Spain.) *Nosotros amamos a nuestra patria.* (We love our country.) *¿A quién vio usted?* (Whom did you see?) *No vi a nadie.* (I didn't see anybody.) But: *Visitaré los Estados Unidos.* (I shall visit the United

States.) Moreover: *Busco un hombre que hable español.* (I am looking for a man who speaks Spanish (indefinite object).)

2. Use *a* before infinitives following verbs of motion, beginning, teaching, learning and a few others: *aprender a,* to learn to; *atreverse a,* to dare to; *ayudar a,* to help to; *comenzar a,* to begin to; *decidirse a,* to decide to; *empezar a,* to begin to; *enseñar a,* to teach to; *invitar a,* to invite to; *ir a,* to go to; *llegar a,* to succeed in; *negarse a,* to deny, to refuse to; *ponerse a,* to begin to; *principiar a,* to begin to; *venir a,* to come to; and *volver a,* (to do something) again: *No me atrevo a ir.* (I don't dare to go.) *Comenzamos (empezamos, principiamos) a comprender.* (We are beginning to understand.) *Mis amigos me invitaron a almorzar.* (My friends invited me to have lunch.) *María fue a visitar a su amiga.* (Mary went to visit her friend.) *Después de comer me puse a estudiar.* (After I had dinner I began to study.) *Haga usted el favor de volver a venir mañana.* (Come back tomorrow, please.) *Me he decidido a ir a España.* (I have decided to go to Spain.)

3. Use *a* with expressions of time: *Le veré a las ocho.* (I shall see you at eight.) *Venga usted a (al) mediodía.* (Come at noon.) *a principios (a mediados, a fines) de mes,* at the start (middle, end) of the month; *a menudo,* often; *a veces,* sometimes, at times.

4. Use *a* to denote the place at which or near which the action of the verb is performed. *Nos sentamos a la mesa.* (We sat at the table.) *Vamos a sentarnos al sol.* (Let us sit in the sun.) *El automóvil está a la puerta.* (The car is at the door.)

5. Use *a* to denote the means, manner, or style in which the governing action is performed: *Vinimos a pie.* (We came on foot (walked).) *Yo no sé escribir a*

máquina. (I can't type.) *Esto está hecho a mano.* (This is handmade.) *a la española,* Spanish style.

6. Use *a* to denote price or quantity: *Se venden a cinco dólares cada una.* (They are sold at five dollars each.) *dos a dos,* two at a time, two by two.

7. Use *a* to denote distance of time or place: *¿A qué distancia está Madrid de aquí? Está a diez kilómetros de aquí.* (How far is Madrid from here? Ten kilometers.) *La casa está a diez minutos de aquí.* (The house is ten minutes from here.) *de Barcelona a Madrid,* from Barcelona to Madrid.

Con

1. Use *con* as you use its English equivalent "with."

2. Use *con* to form such adverbial expressions as: *Hágalo uste con cuidado.* (Do it carefully.) *Él va con frecuencia.* (He goes frequently.)

De

1. Use *de* to denote origin, material of which a thing is made, or point of departure: *María es de España.* (Mary is from Spain.) *Es un reloj de oro.* (It is a gold watch.) *El vapor sale de Nueva York.* (The boat leaves from New York.)

2. Use *de* to denote possession: *La maleta no es mía, es del señor.* (The suitcase does not belong to me, it belongs to that gentleman.) *el sombrero de la señora,* the lady's hat.

3. Use *de* to denote the contents of a receptacle: *Deme usted una taza de café y un vaso de agua.* (Please give me a cup of coffee and a glass of water.)

4. Use *de* to form prepositions from adverbs: *además de,* besides, in addition to; *antes de,* before, in front of; *después de,* after (in time); *detrás de,* behind, in back of.

5. Use *de* with certain verbs before following infinitives: *acabar de,* to have just; to finish; *acordarse de,* to remember to; *alegrarse de,* to be glad to (about), to be happy to (about); *aprovecharse de,* to profit by (from); *cansarse de,* to tire (get tired) of; *cesar de,* to stop; *deber de,* must; (*no*) *dejar de,* (not) to fail to; to stop; *olvidarse de,* to forget to; *quejarse de,* to complain about; *reírse de,* to laugh about; *tratar de,* to try to: *Trate usted de estar a tiempo.* (Try to be on time.) *No me acordé de telefonear.* (I did not remember to telephone.)

Para

1. Use *para* to express the destination for which anything is intended: *Esta carta es para usted.* (This letter is for you.) *¿Para quién es este paquete? Para mí.* (For whom is this package? For me.) *Compré tela para un vestido.* (I bought cloth for a dress.) *Ellos salen para Europa.* (They are leaving for Europe.) *Ella estará allí para el lunes.* (She will be there by Monday.) *Terminaré el trabajo para las cinco.* (I shall finish the work by five o'clock.) *José estudia para médico.* (Joseph is studying to be a doctor.) *El libro fue escrito por el profesor para los alumnos.* (The book was written by the professor for his pupils.)

Por

1. Use *por* to express the agent by whom an action is performed, or to express the course of, source of, or reason for some action: *El libro fue escrito por Cervantes.* (The book was written by Cervantes.) *No compré la casa por falta de dinero.* (I didn't buy the house for lack of money.) *Lo hago por usted.* (I do it for (because of) you (for your sake).) *Vaya usted por mi libro.* (Go after my book.) *Le doy este billete por el*

suyo. (I'll give you this ticket for yours.) *Compré el sombrero por diez dólares.* (I bought the hat for ten dollars.)

2. Use *por* to express duration of time, manner, or means: *Vamos por avión.* (We are going by plane.) *Anduve mucho por las calles.* (I walked the streets a lot.) *Ella va a Chile por un mes.* (She is going to Chile for a month.)

3. Use *por* also in such idiomatic expressions as: *por aquí,* this way; *por completo,* completely; *por lo menos,* at least; *por ejemplo,* for example; *por ahora,* for the present; *por eso,* therefore, for that reason; *por fin,* finally, at last; *por casualidad,* by chance; *por si acaso,* in case, if by chance; *por razones,* for reasons; *por tanto,* therefore; *por lo visto,* apparently; *por todas partes,* everywhere; *por suerte, por fortuna,* fortunately; *por lo general, por lo común,* in general, as a rule.

Hints for Learning the Spanish Verbs

THE PRESENT INDICATIVE

The regular endings of the Present Indicative, First, Second, and Third Conjugations, are:

	First Conjug. -AR verbs	*Second Conjug.* -ER verbs	*Third Conjug.* -IR verbs
Infinitive:	hablar	comer	vivir
Stem:	habl-	com-	viv-
Endings:			
yo	-o	-o	-o
él, ella, usted	-a	-e	-e
nosotros, nosotras	-amos	-emos	-imos
ellos, ellas, ustedes	-an	-en	-en

Observe the endings. The first person singular (*yo*) ends in *-o,* regardless of its stem. *Nosotros* ends in *-mos* (for all verbs and tenses). *Ellos, ellas, ustedes* is made plural by adding *-n* to the singular: *habla, hablan; come, comen; vive, viven.* The only exception to this rule is the verb *ser,* where the third person singular is *es* but the plural is *son.*

There are six verbs whose first person singulars (yo) do not end in *-o:*

dar,	*to give:*	doy	saber,	*to know:*	sé
estar,	*to be:*	estoy	ser,	*to be:*	soy
ir,	*to go:*	voy	haber,	*to have:*	he

THE IMPERFECT INDICATIVE

The regular endings of the Preterite Indicative, First, Second, and Third Conjugations, are:

	First Conjug. -AR verbs	*Second Conjug.* -ER verbs	*Third Conjug.* -IR verbs
Infinitive:	hablar	comer	vivir
Stem:	habl-	com-	viv-
Endings:			
yo	-aba	-ía	-ía
él, ella, usted	-aba	-ía	-ía
nosotros, nosotras	-ábamos	-íamos	-íamos
ellos, ellas, ustedes	-aban	-ían	-ían

The Imperfect Indicative of ALL VERBS is formed by adding the above endings to their respective stems:

hablar:	hablaba	hablaba	hablábamos	hablaban
comer:	comía	comía	comíamos	comían
vivir:	vivía	vivía	vivíamos	vivían

pensar:	pensaba	pensaba	pensábamos	perdían
perder:	perdía	perdía	perdíamos	sentían
sentir:	sentía	sentía	sentíamos	hacían
hacer:	hacía	hacía	hacíamos	pensaban

There are three verbs (and their compounds) which are exceptions to the above rule:

ir:	iba	iba	íbamos	iban
ser:	era	era	éramos	eran
ver:	veía	veía	veíamos	veían

THE PRETERITE (PAST) INDICATIVE

The regular endings of the Imperfect Indicative, First, Second, and Third Conjugations, are:

	First Conjug. -AR verbs	*Second Conjug.* -ER verbs	*Third Conjug.* -IR verbs
Infinitive:	hablar	comer	vivir
Stem:	habl-	com-	viv-
Endings:			
yo	-é	-í	-í
él, ella, usted	-ó	-ió	-ió
nosotros, nosotras	-amos	-imos	-imos
ellos, ellas, ustedes	-aron	-ieron	-ieron

There are seventeen verbs (and their compounds) which are exceptions to the above rule:

andar:	anduve	anduvo	anduvimos	anduvieron
estar:	estuve	estuvo	estuvimos	estuvieron
tener:	tuve	tuvo	tuvimos	tuvieron
caber:	cupe	cupo	cupimos	cupieron
saber:	supe	supo	supimos	supieron

poner:	puse	puso	pusimos	pusieron
querer:	quise	quiso	quisimos	quisieron
haber:	hube	hubo	hubimos	hubieron
hacer:	hice	hizo	hicimos	hicieron
poder:	pude	pudo	pudimos	pudieron
taer:	traje	trajo	trajimos	trajeron
decir:	dije	dijo	dijimos	dijeron
venir:	vine	vino	vinimos	vinieron
conducir:	conduje	condujo	condujimos	condujeron
dar:	di	dio	dimos	dieron
ir:	fui	fue	fuimos	fueron
ser:	fui	fue	fuimos	fueron

THE FUTURE INDICATIVE

The regular endings of the Future Indicative, First, Second, and Third Conjugations, are:

	First Conjug. -AR verbs	*Second Conjug.* -ER verbs	*Third Conjug.* -IR verbs
Infinitive:	hablar	comer	vivir
Stem:	hablar-	comer-	vivir-
Endings:			
yo	-é	-é	-é
él, ella, usted	-á	-á	-á
nosotros, nosotras	-emos	-emos	-emos
ellos, ellas, ustedes	-án	-án	-án

Observe the endings. There is only one set of endings for all verbs, regardless of their stems.

THE CONDITIONAL INDICATIVE

The regular endings of the Conditional Indicative, First, Second, and Third Conjugations, are:

	First Conjug. -AR verbs	*Second Conjug.* -ER verbs	*Third Conjug.* -IR verbs
Infinitive:	hablar	comer	vivir
Stem:	hablar-	comer-	vivir-
Endings:			
yo	-ía	-ía	-ía
él, ella, usted	-ía	-ía	-ía
nosotros, nosotras	-íamos	-íamos	-íamos
ellos, ellas, ustedes	-ían	-ían	-ían

Observe the endings. There is only one set of endings for all verbs, regardless of their stems.

THE PRESENT SUBJUNCTIVE

The easiest and fastest rule for the formation of the Present Subjunctive is as follows: To form the present subjunctive of ALMOST ALL VERBS, drop the ending *-o* of the First Person Singular (*yo*) of the Present Indicative and add the subjunctive endings to their respective stems. The Orthographic (Spelling) Changing Verbs are regular verbs; the spelling change in the stem is made in order to preserve the sound found in the infinitive. Therefore other letters besides *-o* may be omitted and others added before adding the subjunctive endings. The regular endings of the Present Subjunctive, First, Second, and Third Conjugations, are:

	First Conjug. -AR verbs	*Second Conjug.* -ER verbs	*Third Conjug.* -IR verbs
Infinitive:	hablar	comer	vivir

First Person Present:	hablø	comø	vivø
Stem:	habl-	com-	viv-

Endings:			
yo	-e	-a	-a
él, ella, usted	-e	-a	-a
nosotros, nosotras	-emos	-amos	-amos
ellos, ellas, ustedes	-en	-an	-an

Observe the endings. These endings apply to all verbs regardless of their stems. Six verbs and their compounds do not end in *-o* in the First Person Singular of the Present Indicative so their Present Subjunctive can not be formed this way, but their subjunctive endings are the same:

dar	— doy:	dé	dé	demos	den
estar	— estoy:	esté	esté	estemos	estén
ir	— voy:	vaya	vaya	vayamos	vayan
ser	— soy:	sea	sea	seamos	sean
haber	— he:	haya	haya	hayamos	hayan
saber	— sé:	sepa	sepa	sepamos	sepan

THE IMPERFECT SUBJUNCTIVE

The easiest and fastest rule for the formation of the Imperfect Subjunctive is as follows: The Third Person Plural of the Preterite Indicative of ALL VERBS ends in *-ron* (*hablaron, comieron, vivieron, fueron, dijeron, vinieron, pusieron,* etc.). To form the Imperfect Subjunctive of ALL VERBS, drop the ending *-ron* and add the Imperfect Subjunctive endings to the stem. The endings are:

	First Conjug. -AR verbs	Second Conjug. -ER verbs	Third Conjug. -IR verbs
Infinitive:	hablar	comer	vivir
Third Person Preterite:	hablaron	comieron	vivieron
Stem:	habla-	comie-	vivie-

Endings:			
yo	-ra, -se	-ra, -se	-ra, -se
él, ella, usted	-ra, -se	-ra, -se	-ra, -se
nosotros, nosotras	′-ramos, ′-semos	′-ramos, ′-semos	′-ramos, ′-semos
ellos, ellas, ustedes	-ran, -sen	-ran, -sen	-ran, -sen

Observe the endings. There are two sets of endings for the three conjugations. There is no difference between the *-ra* and the *-se* forms. Use either one.

COMMANDS OR IMPERATIVES

The Spanish polite command, often called the "subjunctive used as imperative," is the same, in form, as the present subjunctive (see Commands, below).

THE PRESENT PARTICIPLE

The model verbs (*hablar, comer, vivir*) show how the present participle is formed. The irregular present participles are listed under their corresponding verbs.

THE PAST PARTICIPLE

The model verbs (*hablar, comer, vivir*) show how the past participle is formed. The irregular past participles are listed under their corresponding verbs.

Verb Charts

1. MODEL OF REGULAR VERBS ENDING IN -AR

Simple Tenses—1st Conjugation

INFINITIVE: hablar (*Formed from stem* habl- *and ending* -ar) —to speak

PRESENT PARTICIPLE: hablando (*Infinitive stem and ending* -ando)—speaking

PAST PARTICIPLE: hablado (*Infinitive stem and ending* -ado) —spoken

INDICATIVE MOOD

PRESENT: (*Infinitive stem and endings* -o, -a, -amos, -an)

yo	usted, él, ella	nosotros, nosotras	ustedes, ellos, ellas
hablo	habla	hablamos	hablan

IMPERFECT: (*Infinitive stem and endings* -aba, -aba, ábamos, -aban)

hablaba	hablaba	hablábamos	hablaban

PRETERITE (=PAST): (*Infinitive stem and endings* -é, -ó, -amos, -aron)

hablé	habló	hablamos	hablaron

FUTURE: (*Infinitive and endings* -é, -á, -emos, -án)

hablaré	hablará	hablaremos	hablarán

CONDITIONAL: (*Infinitive and endings* -ía, -ía, -íamos, ían)

hablaría	hablaría	hablaríamos	hablarían

SUBJUNCTIVE MOOD

PRESENT: (*Present indicative 1st person singular. Drop* -o *and add endings* -e, -e, -emos, -en)

hable	hable	hablemos	hablen

IMPERFECT: (*Preterite 3rd person plural. Drop* -ron *and add endings* -ra, -ra, -'ramos, -ran *or* -se, -se, -'semos, -sen)

hablara	hablara	habláramos	hablaran
hablase	hablase	hablásemos	hablasen

IMPERATIVE (=COMMAND): Same forms as Present Subjunctive

2. MODEL OF REGULAR VERBS ENDING IN -ER
Simple Tenses—2nd Conjugation

INFINITIVE: comer (*Formed from stem* com- *and ending* -er) —to eat

PRESENT PARTICIPLE: comiendo (*Infinitive stem and ending* -iendo)—eating

PAST PARTICIPLE: comido (*Infinitive stem and ending* -ido) —eaten

INDICATIVE MOOD

PRESENT: (*Infinitive stem and endings* -o, -e, -emos, -en)

yo	usted, él, ella	nosotros, nosotras	ustedes, ellos, ellas
como	come	comemos	comen

IMPERFECT: (*Infinitive stem and endings* -ía, -ía, -íamos, -ían)

comía	comía	comíamos	comían

PRETERITE (=PAST): (*Infinitive stem and endings* -í, -ió, -imos, -ieron)

comí	comió	comimos	comieron

FUTURE: (*Infinitive and endings* -é, -á, -emos, -án)

comeré	comerá	comeremos	comerán

CONDITIONAL: (*Infinitive and endings* -ía, -ía, -íamos, -ían)

comería	comería	comeríamos	comerían

SUBJUNCTIVE MOOD

PRESENT: (*Present Indicative 1st person singular. Drop* -o *and add endings* -a, -a, -amos, -an)

coma	coma	comamos	coman

IMPERFECT: (*Preterite 3rd person plural. Drop* -ron *and add endings* -ra, -ra, -'ramos, -ran *or* -se, -se, -'semos, -sen)

comiera	comiera	comiéramos	comieran
comiese	comiese	comiésemos	comiesen

IMPERATIVE (=COMMAND): Same forms as Present Subjunctive.

3. MODEL OF REGULAR VERBS ENDING IN -IR

Simple Tenses—3rd Conjugation

INFINITIVE: vivir (*Formed from stem* viv- *and ending* -ir)—to live

PRESENT PARTICIPLE: viviendo (*Infinitive stem and ending* -iendo)—living

PAST PARTICIPLE: vivido (*Infinitive stem and ending* -ido)—lived

INDICATIVE MOOD

PRESENT: (*Infinitive stem and endings* -o, -e, -imos, -en)

yo	usted, él, ella	nosotros, nosotras	ustedes, ellos, ellas
vivo	vive	vivimos	viven

IMPERFECT: (*Infinitive stem and endings* -ía, -ía, -íamos, -ían)

vivía	vivía	vivíamos	vivían

PRETERITE (=PAST): (*Infinitive stem and endings* -í, -ió, -imos, -ieron)

viví	vivió	vivimos	vivieron

FUTURE: (*Infinitive and endings* -é, -á, -emos, -án)

viviré	vivirá	viviremos	vivirán

CONDITIONAL: (*Infinitive and endings* -ía, -ía, -íamos, -ían)

viviría	viviría	viviríamos	vivirían

SUBJUNCTIVE MOOD

PRESENT: (*Present Indicative 1st person singular. Drop* -o *and add endings* -a, -a, -amos, -an)

viva	viva	vivamos	vivan

IMPERFECT: (*Preterite 3rd person plural. Drop* -ron *and add endings* -ra, -ra, -'ramos, -ran *or* -se, -se, -'semos, -sen)

viviera	viviera	viviéramos	vivieran
viviese	viviese	viviésemos	viviesen

IMPERATIVE (=COMMAND): Same forms as Present Subjunctive.

4. MODEL OF PERFECT OR COMPOUND TENSES. Compound tenses are formed with the Irregular Auxiliary Verb *haber* and a past participle (p.p.).

PERFECT INFINITIVE: haber + p.p.—*to have* + p.p.
PERFECT PARTICIPLE: habiendo + p.p.—*having* + p.p.

INDICATIVE MOOD

PRESENT PERFECT:

yo	usted, él, ella	nosotros, nosotras	ustedes, ellos, ellas
he + p.p.	ha + p.p.	hemos + p.p.	han + p.p.

PAST PERFECT (=PLUPERFECT):

había + p.p.	había + p.p.	habíamos + p.p.	habían + p.p.

PRETERITE PERFECT: (*This tense is little used in conversation.*)

hube + p.p.	hubo + p.p.	hubimos + p.p.	hubieron + p.p.

FUTURE PERFECT:

habré + p.p.	habrá + p.p.	habremos + p.p.	habrán + p.p.

CONDITIONAL PERFECT:

habría + p.p.	habría + p.p.	habríamos + p.p.	habrían + p.p.

SUBJUNCTIVE MOOD

PRESENT PERFECT:

haya + p.p.	haya + p.p.	hayamos + p.p.	hayan + p.p.

PAST PERFECT:

hubiera + p.p.	hubiera + p.p.	hubiéramos + p.p.	hubieran + p.p.
hubiese + p.p.	hubiese + p.p.	hubiésemos + p.p.	hubiesen + p.p.

ORTHOGRAPHIC CHANGING VERBS

These verbs are regular; they are conjugated in exactly the same manner as their models: *hablar, comer, vivir.* However, in some tenses they require a slight change in spelling in order to preserve the sound of the final consonant found in the stem. This change occurs only in a few tenses and persons. The others are all regular in spelling.

5. Verbs Ending in *-car*

Change *c* to *qu* before *e*. In this way the sound of *k* is preserved.

buscar—*to look for, to seek:*

Preterite:

busqué, buscó, buscamos, buscaron

Present Subjunctive:

busque,	busque,	busquemos,	busquen

6. Verbs Ending in *-gar*

Change *g* to *gu* before *e*. In this way the hard sound of *g* is preserved.

llegar—*to arrive:*

Preterite:

llegué,	llegó,	llegamos,	llegaron

Present Subjunctive:

llegue,	llegue,	lleguemos,	lleguen

7. Verbs Ending in *-zar*

Change *z* to *c* before *e*. In this way the sound of *th*, or *s*, is preserved. (The letter *z* is seldom used in Spanish before *e*, or *i*.)

gozar—*to enjoy:*

Preterite:

gocé,	gozó,	gozamos,	gozaron

Present Subjunctive:

goce,	goce,	gocemos,	gocen

8. Verbs Ending in *-guar*

The *u* has a diaeresis over it before *e*, indicating that the *u* (*ü*) is pronounced before *e*, or *i*.

averiguar—*to find out:*

Preterite:

averigüé,	averiguó,	averiguamos,	averiguaron

Present Subjunctive:

averigüe,	averigüe,	averigüemos,	averigüen

9. Verbs Ending in *-ger* and *-gir*

Change *g* to *j* before *a* or *o*. In this way the aspirated sound of the *g* is preserved.

coger—*to catch, to pick:*
dirigir—*to direct:*

Present Indicative:

cojo,	coge,	cogemos,	cogen
dirijo,	dirige,	dirigimos,	dirigen

Present Subjunctive:

coja,	coja,	cojamos,	cojan
dirija,	dirija,	dirijamos,	dirijan

10. Verbs Ending in *-guir*

Change *gu* to *g* before *o* or *a*. The letter *u* is not pronounced in the combination *gui* (or *gue*), but is pronounced in the combination *gua* or *guo*.

distinguir—*to distinguish:*

Present Indicative:

distingo,	distingue,	distinguimos,	distinguen

Present Subjunctive:

distinga,	distinga,	distingamos,	distingan

11. Verbs Ending in *-cer* (and *-cir*)

Change the *c* to *z* before *a* or *o*. In this way the soft sound of the *c* is preserved. Note: Verbs in *-cer* and *-cir* have the above changes when the *c* of *-cer* and *-cir* is preceded by a consonant.

vencer—*to overcome:*

Present Indicative:

venzo,	vence,	vencemos,	vencen

Present Subjunctive:

venza,	venza,	venzamos,	venzan

12. Verbs Ending in *-cer* (and *-cir*)

Insert *z* before *c* when *c* is followed by an ending beginning with *a* or *o*. Verbs in *-cer* and *-cir* have the above insertion when the *c* of *-cer* and *-cir* is preceded by a vowel. (See *conducir* below.)

conocer—*to know:*

Present Indicative:

conozco,	conoce,	conocemos,	conocen

Present Subjunctive:

conozca,	conozca,	conozcamos,	conozcan

13. Verbs Ending in *-ducir*

Insert *z* before *c* when *c* is followed by an ending beginning with *a* or *o*. In the preterite and imperfect subjunctive the *c* changes to *j* and the *i* of the ending is dropped.

conducir—*to conduct:*

Present Indicative:

conduzco,	conduce,	conducimos,	conducen

Present Subjunctive:

conduzca,	conduzca,	conduzcamos,	conduzcan

Preterite:

conduje,	condujo,	condujimos,	condujeron

Imperfect Subjunctive:

condujera,	condujera,	condujéramos,	condujeran
condujese,	condujese,	condujésemos,	condujesen

VERBS WITH STEMS ENDING IN A VOWEL

14. Some Verbs Ending in *-iar* and *-uar*

Some of the verbs with these endings stress the final *i* or *u* of the stem and must, therefore, have a written accent over the *i* or *u*.

enviar—*to send:*
continuar—*to continue, to go on:*

Present Indicative:

envío,	envía,	enviamos,	envían
continúo,	continúa,	continuamos,	continúan

Present Subjunctive:

envíe,	envíe,	enviemos,	envíen
continúe,	continúe,	continuemos,	continúen

15. Verbs Ending in *-eer*

Change the unstressed *i* to *y* when it occurs between vowels in order to conform to the rules of good sound (euphony).

leer—*to read:*

Present Participle:
leyendo
Past Participle:
leído
Preterite:

leí,	leyó,	leímos,	leyeron

Imperfect Subjunctive:

leyera,	leyera,	leyéramos,	leyeran
leyese,	leyese,	leyésemos,	leyesen

16. Verbs Ending in *-uir*

Verbs ending in *-uir* (but not *-guir*) change the unstressed *i* to *y* when it occurs between vowels; and *y* is inserted before *a, o, e.*

huir—*to flee, to run away:*

Present Participle:
huyendo
Present Indicative:

huyo,	huye,	huimos,	huyen

Preterite:

hui,	huyó,	huimos,	huyeron

Present Subjunctive:

huya,	huya,	huyamos,	huyan

Imperfect Subjunctive:

huyera,	huyera,	huyéramos,	huyeran
huyese,	huyese,	huyésemos,	huyesen

RADICAL CHANGING VERBS

These verbs change the last vowel of the stem when the stress falls on that syllable. Change *e* to *ie* and *o* to *ue*. This category includes *-ar* and *-er* verbs only. Only the irregular persons and tenses are given; the tenses not listed are regular. The following verbs serve as models.

17. Change *e* to *ie.*

pensar—*to think:*

Present Indicative:

pienso,	piensa,	pensamos,	piensan

Present Subjunctive:

piense,	piense,	pensemos,	piensen

18. Change *e* to *ie.*

perder—*to lose:*

Present Indicative:

pierdo,	pierde,	perdemos,	pierden

Present Subjunctive:

pierda,	pierda,	perdamos,	pierdan

19. Change *o* to *ue*. The verb *jugar*—to play (a game)—is also in this category; the *u* changes to *ue*.

contar—*to count:*

Present Indicative:
cuento, cuenta, contamos, cuentan
Present Subjunctive:
cuente, cuente, contemos, cuenten

20. Change *o* to *ue*. The verb *oler*—to smell—is also in this category, except that initial *ue* is spelled *hue: huelo, huele,* etc., but, *olemos; olí,* etc.

volver—*to return, to go (come) back:*

Present Indicative:
vuelvo, vuelve, volvemos, vuelven
Present Subjunctive:
vuelva, vuelva, volvamos, vuelvan

The following verbs change the last vowel of the stem when the stress falls on that syllable. Change *e* to *ie* and *o* to *ue*. Change unstressed *e* to *i* and *o* to *u* when followed in the next syllable by *a, ie, io*. This category includes *-ir* verbs only.

21. Change *e* to *ie* and *e* to *i*.

sentir—*to feel, to be sorry:*

Present Participle:
sintiendo
Present Indicative:
siento, siente, sentimos, sienten

Present Subjunctive:
sienta, sienta, sintamos, sientan
Preterite:
sentí, sintió, sentimos, sintieron
Imperfect Subjunctive:
sintiera, sintiera, sintiéramos, sintieran
sintiese, sintiese, sintiésemos, sintiesen

22. Change *o* to *ue* and *o* to *u*.

dormir—*to sleep:*

Present Participle:
durmiendo
Present Indicative:
duermo, duerme, dormimos, duermen
Present Subjunctive:
duerma, duerma, durmamos, duerman
Preterite:
dormí, durmió, dormimos, durmieron
Imperfect Subjunctive:
durmiera, durmiera, durmiéramos, durmieran
durmiese, durmiese, durmiésemos, durmiesen

The following verbs change the last vowel of the stem when the stress falls on that syllable. Change *e* to *i*. Change unstressed *e* to *i* when followed in the next syllable by *a, ie, io*. This category includes *-ir* verbs only.

23. Change *e* to *i*.

pedir—*to ask, to ask for:*

Present Participle:
pidiendo

Present Indicative:

pido,	pide,	pedimos,	piden

Present Subjunctive:

pida,	pida,	pidamos,	pidan

Preterite:

pedí,	pidió,	pedimos,	pidieron

Imperfect Subjunctive:

pidiera,	pidiera,	pidiéramos,	pidieran
pidiese,	pidiese,	pidiésemos,	pidiesen

24. Change *e* to *i*.

reír—*to laugh:*

Present Participle:

riendo

Present Indicative:

río,	ríe,	reímos,	ríen

Present Subjunctive:

ría,	ría,	riamos,	rían

Preterite:

reí,	rio,	reímos,	rieron

Imperfect Subjunctive:

riera,	riera,	riéramos,	rieran
riese,	riese,	riésemos,	riesen

INFIN.	PARTICIP. IMPERAT.	PRES. INDIC.	IMPERF. INDIC.	PRET. INDIC.
25.	andando			
	andado	ando	andaba	anduve
andar		anda	andaba	anduvo
to walk	ande	andamos	andábamos	anduvimos
	andemos	andan	andaban	anduvieron
	anden			
26.	cabiendo			
	cabido	quepo	cabía	cupe
caber		cabe	cabía	cupo
to fit,	quepa	cabemos	cabíamos	cupimos
to be room	quepamos	caben	cabían	cupieron
(for)	quepan			
27.	cayendo			
	caído	caigo	caía	caí
caer		cae	caía	cayó
to fall	caiga	caemos	caíamos	caímos
	caigamos	caen	caían	cayeron
	caigan			
28.	dando			
	dado	doy	daba	di
dar		da	daba	dio
to give	dé	damos	dábamos	dimos
	demos	dan	daban	dieron
	den			

IRREGULAR VERBS

FUT. INDIC.	CONDIT. INDIC.	PRES. SUBJUNCT.	IMPERF. SUBJUNCT.	
andaré	andaría	ande	anduviera	anduviese
andará	andaría	ande	anduviera	anduviese
andaremos	andaríamos	andemos	anduviéramos	anduviésemos
andarán	andarían	anden	anduvieran	anduviesen
cabré	cabría	quepa	cupiera	cupiese
cabrá	cabría	quepa	cupiera	cupiese
cabremos	cabríamos	quepamos	cupiéramos	cupiésemos
cabrán	cabrían	quepan	cupieran	cupiesen
caeré	caería	caiga	cayera	cayese
caerá	caería	caiga	cayera	cayese
caeremos	caeríamos	caigamos	cayéramos	cayésemos
caerán	caerían	caigan	cayeran	cayesen
daré	daría	dé	diera	diese
dará	daría	dé	diera	diese
daremos	daríamos	demos	diéramos	diésemos
darán	darían	den	dieran	diesen

IRREGULAR VERBS

INFIN.	PARTICIP. IMPERAT.	PRES. INDIC.	IMPERF. INDIC.	PRET. INDIC.
29.	diciendo			
	dicho	digo	decía	dije
decir		dice	decía	dijo
to say,	diga	decimos	decíamos	dijimos
to tell	digamos	dicen	decían	dijeron
	digan			
30.	estando			
	estado	estoy	estaba	estuve
estar		está	estaba	estuvo
to be	esté	estamos	estábamos	estuvimos
	estemos	están	estaban	estuvieron
	estén			
31.	habiendo			
	habido	he	había	hube
haber		ha	había	hubo
to have		hemos	habíamos	hubimos
		han	habían	hubieron
32.	haciendo			
	hecho	hago	hacía	hice
hacer		hace	hacía	hizo
to do,	haga	hacemos	hacíamos	hicimos
to make	hagamos	hacen	hacían	hicieron
	hagan			

IRREGULAR VERBS

FUT. INDIC.	CONDIT. INDIC.	PRES. SUBJUNCT.	IMPERFEC. SUBJUNCT.	
diré	diría	diga	dijera	dijese
dirá	diría	diga	dijera	dijese
diremos	diríamos	digamos	dijéramos	dijésemos
dirán	dirían	digan	dijeran	dijesen
estaré	estaría	esté	estuviera	estuviese
estará	estaría	esté	estuviera	estuviese
estaremos	estaríamos	estemos	estuviéramos	estuviésemos
estarán	estarían	estén	estuvieran	estuviesen
habré	habría	haya	hubiera	hubiese
habrá	habría	haya	hubiera	hubiese
habremos	habríamos	hayamos	hibiéramos	hubiésemos
habrán	habrían	hayan	hubieran	hubiesen
haré	haría	haga	hiciera	hiciese
hará	haría	haga	hiciera	hiciese
haremos	haríamos	hagamos	hiciéramos	hiciésemos
harán	harían	hagan	hicieran	hiciesen

INFIN.	PARTICIP. IMPERAT.	PRES. INDIC.	IMPERF. INDIC.	PRET. INDIC.
33.	yendo			
	ido	voy	iba	fui
ir		va	iba	fue
to go	vaya	vamos	íbamos	fuimos
	vayamos	van	iban	fueron
	vayan			
34.	oyendo			
	oído	oigo	oía	oí
oír		oye	oía	oyó
to hear	oiga	oímos	oíamos	oímos
	oigamos	oyen	oían	oyeron
	oigan			
35.	pudiendo			
	podido	puedo	podía	pude
poder		puede	podía	pudo
to be able	pueda	podemos	podíamos	pudimos
	podamos	pueden	podían	pudieron
	puedan			
36.	poniendo			
	puesto	pongo	ponía	puse
poner		pone	ponía	puso
to put	ponga	ponemos	poníamos	pusimos
	pongamos	ponen	ponían	pusieron
	pongan			

IRREGULAR VERBS

FUT. INDIC.	CONDIT. INDIC.	PRES. SUBJUNCT.	IMPERFEC. SUBJUNCT.	
iré	iría	vaya	fuera	fuese
irá	iría	vaya	fuera	fuese
iremos	iríamos	vayamos	fuéramos	fuésemos
irán	irían	vayan	fueran	fuesen
oiré	oiría	oiga	oyera	oyese
oirá	oiría	oiga	oyera	oyese
oiremos	oiríamos	oigamos	oyéramos	oyésemos
oirán	oirían	oigan	oyeran	oyesen
podré	podría	pueda	pudiera	pudiese
podrá	podría	pueda	pudiera	pudiese
podremos	podríamos	podamos	pudiéramos	pudiésemos
podrán	podrían	puedan	pudieran	pudiesen
pondré	pondría	ponga	pusiera	pusiese
pondrá	pondría	ponga	pusiera	pusiese
pondremos	pondríamos	pongamos	pusiéramos	pusiésemos
pondrán	pondrían	pongan	pusieran	pusiesen

INFIN.	PARTICIP. IMPERAT.	PRES. INDIC.	IMPERF. INDIC.	PRET. INDIC.
37.	queriendo			
	querido	quiero	quería	quise
querer		quiere	quería	quiso
to want,	quiera	queremos	queríamos	quisimos
to wish	queramos	quieren	querían	quisieron
	quieran			
38.	sabiendo			
	sabido	sé	sabía	supe
saber		sabe	sabía	supo
to know	sepa	sabemos	sabíamos	supimos
	sepamos	saben	sabían	supieron
	sepan			
39.	saliendo			
	salido	salgo	salía	salí
salir		sale	salía	salió
to leave,	salga	salimos	salíamos	salimos
to go (come)	salgamos	salen	salían	salieron
out	salgan			
40.	siendo			
	sido	soy	era	fui
ser		es	era	fue
to be	sea	somos	éramos	fuimos
	seamos	son	eran	fueron
	sean			

FUT. INDIC.	CONDIT. INDIC.	PRES. SUBJUNCT.	IMPERFEC. SUBJUNCT.	
querré	querría	quiera	quisiera	quisiese
querrá	querría	quiera	quisiera	quisiese
querremos	querríamos	queramos	quisiéramos	quisiésemos
querrán	querrían	quieran	quisieran	quisiesen
sabré	sabría	sepa	supiera	supiese
sabrá	sabría	sepa	supiera	supiese
sabremos	sabríamos	sepamos	supiéramos	supiésemos
sabrán	sabrían	sepan	supieran	supiesen
saldré	saldría	salga	saliera	saliese
saldrá	saldría	salga	saliera	saliese
saldremos	saldríamos	salgamos	saliéramos	saliésemos
saldrán	saldrían	salgan	salieran	saliesen
seré	sería	sea	fuera	fuese
será	sería	sea	fuera	fuese
seremos	seríamos	seamos	fuéramos	fuésemos
serán	serían	sean	fueran	fuesen

INFIN.	PARTICIP. IMPERAT.	PRES. INDIC.	IMPERF. INDIC.	PRET. INDIC.
41.	teniendo			
	tenido	tengo	tenía	tuve
tener		tiene	tenía	tuvo
to have	tenga	tenemos	teníamos	tuvimos
	tengamos	tienen	tenían	tuvieron
	tengan			
42.	trayendo			
	traído	traigo	traía	traje
traer		trae	traía	trajo
to bring	traiga	traemos	traíamos	trajimos
	traigamos	traen	traían	trajeron
	traigan			
43.	valiendo			
	valido	valgo	valía	valí
valer		vale	valía	valió
to cost,	valga	valemos	valíamos	valimos
to be worth	valgamos	valen	valían	valieron
	valgan			
44.	viniendo			
	venido	vengo	venía	vine
venir		viene	venía	vino
to come	venga	venimos	veníamos	vinimos
	vengamos	vienen	venían	vinieron
	vengan			

IRREGULAR VERBS

FUT. INDIC.	CONDIT. INDIC.	PRES. SUBJUNCT.	IMPERFEC. SUBJUNCT.	
tendré	tendría	tenga	tuviera	tuviese
tendrá	tendría	tenga	tuviera	tuviese
tendremos	tendríamos	tengamos	tuviéramos	tuviésemos
tendrán	tendrían	tengan	tuvieran	tuviesen
traeré	traería	traiga	trajera	trajese
traerá	traería	traiga	trajera	trajese
traeremos	traeríamos	traigamos	trajéramos	trajésemos
traerán	traerían	traigan	trajeran	trajesen
valdré	valdría	valga	valiera	valiese
valdrá	valdría	valga	valiera	valiese
valdremos	valdríamos	valgamos	valiéramos	valiésemos
valdrán	valdrían	valgan	valieran	valiesen
vendré	vendría	venga	viniera	viniese
vendrá	vendría	venga	viniera	viniese
vendremos	vendríamos	vengamos	viniéramos	viniésemos
vendrán	vendrían	vengan	vinieran	viniesen

INFIN.	PARTICIP. IMPERAT.	PRES. INDIC.	IMPERF. INDIC.	PRET. INDIC.
45.	viendo			
	visto	veo	veía	vi
ver		ve	veía	vio
to see	vea	vemos	veíamos	vimos
	veamos	ven	veían	vieron
	vean			

Ser

The verb *ser,* like *estar,* corresponds to "to be" in English.

1. Use *ser* with predicate nouns and pronouns: *El señor es médico.* (The gentleman is a doctor.). *Ellos son comerciantes.* (They are businessmen.). *El profesor es español.* (The professor is a Spaniard.). *La capital de España es Madrid.* (The capital of Spain is Madrid.). *Son los niños.* (It is the children.). *Soy yo.* (It is I.). *¿Es usted, María?* (Is it you, Maria?)

2. Use *ser* with nouns denoting origin, material of which a thing is made, and ownership: *El caballero es de Colombia.* (The gentleman is from Colombia.). *La mesa es de madera.* (The table is made of wood.). *Esta maleta es de la señora.* (This suitcase belongs to the lady.)

Use *ser* with impersonal and time expressions: *Es urgente que usted salga en seguida.* (It is urgent that you leave at once.). *No es importante comprarlo.* (It

FUT. INDIC.	CONDIT. INDIC.	PRES. SUBJUNCT.	IMPERFEC. SUBJUNCT.	
veré	vería	vea	viera	viese
verá	vería	vea	viera	viese
veremos	veríamos	veamos	viéramos	viésemos
verán	verían	vean	vieran	viesen

is not important to buy it.). *Es tarde (temprano).* (It is late (early).). *Es verano.* (It is summer.). *Es la una.* (It is one o'clock.). *Son las dos (las tres,* etc.). (It is two (three, etc.) o'clock.). *Hoy es lunes.* (Today is Monday.)

4. Use *ser* with predicate adjectives denoting INHERENT or CHARACTERISTIC qualities of the subject. These include character, appearance, color, size, shape, age and financial condition. Age (*joven,* young; *viejo,* old) and financial condition (*rico,* rich; *pobre,* poor) are felt to describe personal qualities: *El niño es bueno.* (The boy is good.). *La niña es linda.* (The girl is pretty.). *La camisa es blanca.* (The shirt is white.). *El cuarto es grande.* (The room is large.). *La mesa es redonda.* (The table is round.). *Mi padre es viejo.* (My father is old.). *Mi hermana es joven.* (My sister is young.). *José es rico, pero María es pobre.* (José is rich, but Maria is poor.)

5. Use *ser* + the past participle to form the passive voice (see Voice, below).

Estar

1. Use *estar* with predicate adjectives (and past participles used as adjectives) denoting STATE OR CONDITION which is not inherent in or characteristic of the subject: *¿Cómo está usted? Estoy bien, gracias.* (How are you? I am well, thank you.). *La niña está buena (bien), pero el niño está malo (enfermo).* (The girl is well, but the boy is sick.). *Estoy muy cansado.* (I am very tired.). *Los niños anduvieron mucho y ahora están cansados.* (The children walked a lot and now they are very tired.). *El agua está fría, pero el café está caliente.* (The water is cold, but the coffee is hot.). *La puerta está cerrada.* (The door is closed.). *El libro está cerrado.* (The book is closed.). *Las tiendas y los bancos están cerrados los domingos.* (The stores and the banks are closed on Sundays.). *El presidente está muerto* (to be dead or alive is felt to be a state or condition, not an inherent or characteristic quality). (The president is dead.)

2. Use *estar* also to express position or location: *Ellos no están aquí.* (They are not here.). *El sombrero está en el sofá.* (The hat is on the sofa.). *El profesor está ahora en España.* (The professor is now in Spain.). *Caracas está en Venezuela.* (Caracas is in Venezuela.). *Venezuela está en Sud América.* (Venezuela is in South America.)

Voice

Voice tells whether the subject of the (transitive) verb acts or is acted upon. Active voice denotes that the subject of the verb is the actor: *José escribió el libro.* (José wrote the book.). *Maria cerró la puerta.* (Maria closed the door.). Passive voice denotes that the subject of the verb is the receiver of the action: *El libro fue escrito por José.* (The book was written by José.). *La puerta fue cerrada por María.* (The door was closed by Maria.) A verb whose past participle is used with any tense of *ser* is said to be in the passive voice. When past participles are used with *ser,* or *estar,* they agree in gender and number with the words to which they relate. Past participles with *haber* never change their ending *-o.*

The English "by," preceded by the passive voice, is translated by *por* when the action is physical, and by *de* when the action is mental: *América fue descubierta por Cristóbal Colón.* (America was discovered by Christopher Columbus.). *Abraham Lincoln es admirado y respetado de todos.* (Abraham Lincoln is admired and respected by all.)

When the actor or agent of the action is not expressed, the passive voice may also be used: *Los libros fueron vendidos.* (The books were sold.) Spanish-speaking people, however, prefer a reflexive—*se* + the verb in the third person—or a verb in the third person plural: *Se vendieron los libros.* (The books were sold.). *Aquí se habla español* or, *Aquí hablan español.* (Spanish is spoken here.)

The English indefinite "one," "you," "they," "people," etc., + an active verb, or the impersonal passive formed with "it," may also be expressed in Spanish by the above forms: *Se dice que ella llegará mañana,* or *Dicen que ella llegará mañana.* (It is said that she will arrive tomorrow.). *¿Cómo se dice eso en español?* (How does one say that in Spanish?) In these expressions, an indirect object pronoun may be placed between *se* and the verb to indicate the person to whom something has been said, done, etc.: *Se me dice que ella llegará mañana.* (I am told that she will arrive tomorrow.)

Estar + a past participle does not form the passive voice. It is used not to describe an action, which *ser* + a past participle does, but to describe a situation or stationary condition: *La puerta estaba cerrada cuando llegué.* (The door was closed when I arrived.). *Las ventanas estaban abiertas* (*y yo las cerré porque hacía mucho frío*). (The windows were open (and I closed them because it was too cold.). *La casa está rodeada de un bello jardín.* (The house is surrounded by a beautiful garden.) Note that *de,* not *por,* is used to describe a stationary condition.

The Uses of the Tenses

THE INFINITIVE

1. Translate "on" (when, upon) + a present participle into Spanish as *al* + the infinitive: *Al salir de casa esta mañana, vi a Elena.* (On leaving my house this morning, I saw Elena.)

2. Use infinitives as verbal nouns preceded by *el: El viajar es agradable.* (Traveling is pleasant.)

3. Use infinitives as objects of prepositions: *Le telefonearé a usted antes de ir a su despacho.* (I shall telephone you before I go to your office.). *Ellos salieron sin despedirse.* (They left without saying good-bye.)

THE PRESENT PARTICIPLE

A present participle never changes its *-o* ending.

1. Use present participles after forms of *estar* (to

be) to form progressive tenses (Spanish does not use this tense as much as English for it limits action to time specified, either expressed or understood): *Estoy escribiendo a mis padres* (*ahora*). (I am writing to my parents (now).). *Estuve estudiando anoche.* (I was studying last night.). *Estaba leyendo cuando él llegó.* (I was reading when he arrived.) Don't use the progressive with verbs of motion; use the present tense instead: *Voy a casa.* (I am going home.). *María viene esta noche.* (Maria is coming tonight.)

2. Use present participles after the verbs *seguir* (to continue, to go on) and *continuar* (to continue): *Continúe* (*siga*) *usted leyendo.* (Go on reading.)

3. Don't translate "by" when it is used with the present participle; use the present participle alone in Spanish: *Se aprende estudiando.* (One learns by studying.)

THE PAST PARTICIPLE

Past participles used with *haber* never change their *-o* endings.

1. Use past participles after forms of the auxiliary verb *haber* (to have) to form the perfect tense: *¿Ha abierto usted la ventana?* (Have you opened the window?). *¿Han visto ustedes mis libros?* (Have you seen my books?) Don't place any word between *haber* and the past participle.

2. With few exceptions the perfect tense is used as in English (see The Present Tense, 3, below), and, as in English, this tense is often equivalent to the simple past: *He hablado con María,* or *Hablé con María.* (I have spoken to Maria, or, I spoke to Maria.) Don't confuse *haber* with *tener,* which also means "to have"; *tener* is used to denote possession.

3. Past participles not used with *haber* agree, like

other adjectives, with the words to which they refer: *La ventana fué abierta por José* (see *Ser*, 5, above). (The window was opened by José.). *La ventana estaba abierta cuando llegué* (see *Estar*, 1, above). (The window was open when I arrived.)

THE PRESENT TENSE

1. Translate "I speak, I do speak, I am speaking" by *yo hablo* (see The Present Participle, 1, above).

2. Use the present tense instead of the future when you ask for simple directions or instructions. "Will" meaning "willing to" is translated by *querer* followed by an infinitive: *¿Quiere usted ir conmigo?* (Will you go with me?). *Hace usted el favor de* (or *¿Quiere usted*) *decirme dónde está el hotel Ritz?* (Will you please tell me where the Ritz hotel is?). *¿Dónde pongo las maletas?* (Where shall I put the suitcases?). *¿Pago ahora?* (Shall I pay now?)

3. Use the present tense instead of the present perfect to describe an action beginning in the past and continuing to the present: *Hace* + an expression of time + *que* + the present tense of the verb: *¿Cuánto tiempo hace que está usted en Caracas? Hace ocho días que estoy aquí.* (How long have you been in Caracas? I have been here for a week.) The statement may be transposed and *que* omitted: *Estoy aquí hace ocho días.* When asking for a more specific time, use *desde* + days, months, etc.: *¿Desde cuándo está en Caracas? Estoy aquí desde el lunes.* (How long (since when) have you been (are you) in Caracas? I have been (am) here since Monday.). *¿Desde cuándo no ve usted a María? No la veo desde abril.* (When did you last see Maria? I haven't seen her since April.)

4. Translate "ago" by *hace* + a time expression +

que + the past tense of the verb: *Hace un mes que llegué.* (I arrived a month ago.) The statement may be transposed and *que* omitted: *Llegué hace un mes.*

5. Use the present tense instead of the past with the expressions *por poco* and *casi* (almost): *Por poco compro el automóvil.* (I almost bought the automobile.)

THE PAST, OR PRETERITE, TENSE

This tense denotes a past, completed action (see The Imperfect Tense, 6, below): *Yo hablé con mi padre.* (I spoke with my father.). *Mi hermana fue a la tienda.* (My sister went to the store.). *Ellos llegaron anoche.* (They arrived last night.)

THE IMPERFECT TENSE

1. Use the imperfect to describe a repeated or customary action or state in the past. This past action or state may be expressed in English by "was" or "were," "used to," or "would": *Cuando era niño vivía en San Sebastián.* (When I was a boy I used to live in San Sebastián.). *Usted estaba en Buenos Aires cuando yo estaba en Lima.* (You were in Buenos Aires when I was in Lima.). *Yo la veía a menudo, pero ahora no la veo.* (I used to see her often, but I do not see her now.). *A menudo salía sin mí.* (She would often go out without me.)

2. The verbs *conocer,* "to know"; *creer,* "to think," "to believe"; *deber,* "to have to (must, should, ought)"; *pensar,* "to think"; *querer,* "to wish," "to want"; *saber,* "to know"; *sentirse,* "to feel"; *temer,* "to fear"; and *tener,* "to have," are generally used in the imperfect instead of in the simple past (preterite) when the state or condition prevailed in the past for some time: *Yo creía que José estaba en México.* (I

thought José was in Mexico.). *Ellos no sabían que yo estaba en Nueva York.* (They did not know I was in New York.). *No la conocía, pero la conozco ahora.* (I did not know her, but I know her now.)

3. An action that was going on when something else happened may be expressed by an imperfect followed by a simple past (preterite): *Yo leía cuando él entró,* or *Yo estaba leyendo cuando él entró.* (I was reading when he came in.). *¿Adónde iba usted cuando la vi?* (Where were you going when I saw you?). *¿Qué hacía usted cuando la llamé por teléfono?* (What were you doing when I telephoned you?)

4. Use the imperfect to describe someone or something so as to recognize or identify him or it: *Nuestro padre era alto, fuerte, y bondadoso.* (Our father was tall, strong, and kind.)

5. Use the imperfect instead of the past perfect to describe an action beginning in the past and continuing to a certain stated time in the past (see The Present Tense, 3, above). *Hacía una hora que le esperaba cuando llegó.* (I had been waiting for an hour when he arrived.). *No hacía mucho tiempo que estaba en Madrid cuando recibí una postal de ellos.* (I had not been in Madrid long when I received a postcard from them.)

6. Use the imperfect to tell time in the past: *¿Qué hora era cuando me telefoneó usted?* (What time was it when you telephoned me?). *Eran las tres de la tarde.* (It was three o'clock in the afternoon.)

THE FUTURE TENSE

1. Use the future tense to describe action in the future just as English uses "shall" or "will" (see The Present Tense, 2, above): *Mañana compraré todo lo que necesito.* (Tomorrow I shall buy everything I

need.). *Iremos el lunes.* (We shall go on Monday.). *Ellos saldrán el mes que viene.* (They will leave next month.). *Guillermo irá por vapor y volverá por avión.* (William will go by boat and return by plane.). *Estoy diciéndole a mi padre que saldré temprano.* (I am telling my father that I shall leave early.). *José dice que irá mañana.* (José says that he will go tomorrow.). *Ella escribe que no vendrá.* (She writes that she will not come.)

2. Use the future tense to express probability or supposition in present time. This idea may be expressed in English by "wonder," "must," "can," "probably," or "suppose": *¿Qué hora será?* (I wonder what time is it? or, What time do you suppose it is? or, What time can it be?). *Será la una.* (It is probably one o'clock, or, It must be one o'clock.). *¿Dónde estará María?* (I wonder where Maria is?)

3. Use the present of *ir + a,* just as English uses the present progressive of "to go" to express idiomatic future: *Voy a comprar cigarrillos.* (I am going to (will) buy cigarettes.)

THE CONDITIONAL TENSE

Use the conditional tense to describe an action dating from the past just as English uses "should" or "would" (see The Imperfect Tense, 1, above): *Le dije a mi padre que saldría temprano.* (I told my father that I would leave early.). *José dijo que iría mañana.* (José said that he would go tomorrow.). *Ella escribió que no vendría.* (She wrote that she would not come.). *Me dijo que lo haría si podía* (see Conditional Sentences, 1, Note, below). (He told me that he would do it if he could.)

2. Use the conditional to express probability or supposition in past time (see The Future Tense, 2,

above): *¿Qué hora sería cuando llegó José?* (I wonder what time it was when José arrived, or, What time do you suppose it was when José arrived?). *Sería la una cuando llegó.* (It was probably one o'clock when he arrived.). *¿Dónde estaría María anoche?* (I wonder where Maria was last night.)

3. Use the conditional tense when "should" or "would" expresses a desire or a polite request (see The Present Tense, 2, above, and The Imperfect Subjunctive, 5, below): *Me gustaría comprar la casa pero no me atrevo.* (I would (should) like to buy the house but I don't dare.). *A María le gustaría ir conmigo pero no puede.* (Maria would like to go with me but she can't.). *Me alegraría (de) conocerla.* (I would (should) be glad to meet her.)

4. When "should" means "ought to," use *deber: Usted debería ir allí.* (You should go there.)

Commands, or Imperatives

Spanish polite command is the same in form as the present subjunctive (this book does not use the familiar command or any other familiar form).

1. Use *usted* and *ustedes* after a direct command. You may also use *por favor* after *usted* and *ustedes,* but it is not essential. When we include ourselves in the command ("let us"), *nosotros* or *nosotras* is generally omitted: *Hable usted en español, por favor.* (Speak Spanish, please.). *Hábleme usted en español, por favor.* (Speak to me in Spanish, please.). *Háblenme ustedes en español.* (Speak to me in Spanish.). *Háblenos usted en español.* (Speak to us in Spanish.). *Hablemos en español.* (Let's speak Spanish.). *Escribamos estas cartas.* (Let's write these letters.). *Escriba usted*

la carta. (Write the letter, please.). *Lea usted en voz alta, no lea en voz baja.* (Please read right out loud, don't read in a low tone.)

2. Another common command form for "let us" is *vamos a* + the verb or noun: *Vamos a ver.* (Let's see.). *Vamos a leer.* (Let's read.). *Vamos a pasear.* (Let's take a walk.). *Vamos al museo.* (Let's go to the museum.)

3. Reflexive affirmative commands are formed from the first person plural by dropping the *-s* and adding the reflexive pronoun *nos;* negatives retain the *-s* and do not invert: *Lavémonos,* or *Vamos a lavarnos.* (Let's wash.). *No nos lavemos.* (Let's not wash.). *Sentémonos aquí,* or *Vamos a sentarnos aquí.* (Let's sit down here.). *No nos sentemos aquí.* (Let's not sit here.) Note: The affirmative command of *ir* is: *¡Vamos!* or *¡Vámonos!* (Let's go!) The negative is: *No vayamos,* or *No nos vayamos.* (Let's not go.)

4. In indirect commands, "let" is translated by *que* + the command: *Que pase.* (Let him come in.). *Que pasen.* (Let them come in.). *Que vaya ahora mismo.* (Let him go right away.)

5. In direct commands, "let" (allow, permit) is translated by the command forms of *dejar* and *permitir,* and sometimes by the indicative of these two verbs: *Déjeme usted ver eso.* (Let me see that.). *Déjenos usted en paz.* (Let us alone.). *¿Me deja usted ver eso?* (Will you let me see that?). *¡Nos deja usted en paz!* (Will you let us alone!)

The Subjunctives

THE PRESENT SUBJUNCTIVE

1. Use the subjunctive when the subject of the verb

in the main clause is different from the subject of the verb in the dependent clause; that is, when I want you to do something, or you want me to do something: *Yo quiero que usted hable español.* (I want you to speak Spanish.). *Usted quiere que yo hable español.* (You want me to speak Spanish.). *Ellos quieren que nosotros hablemos español.* (They want us to speak Spanish.) Note: When the subjects of the two verbs are the same, that is, when I want to do something myself, use the infinitive, not the subjunctive: *Yo quiero hablar español.* (I want to speak Spanish.). *Usted quiere hablar español.* (You want to speak Spanish.). *Ellos quieren hablar español.* (They want to speak Spanish.)

2. To use the present subjunctive, simple or compound, in the dependent clause, the verb in the main clause must be in the present or future indicative (simple or compound), or in a command form, and the verb must express "volition" (will), emotion or feeling, belief, doubt or denial. The subject pronouns are used to help you, but in conversation we know to whom we are referring and therefore they are not essential. You may grasp the idea of the subjunctive more easily by recalling that in English the subjunctive is similarly used in many expressions: It is my wish that she wait here (*not* waits). In Spanish: *Yo quiero que ella espere aquí.* To illustrate at some length: *¿Quiere usted que yo lea?* (Do you want me to read?). *Ellos desean que usted salga temprano.* (They want you to leave early.). *Yo temo que Elena no venga.* (I am afraid Elena will not come.). *Yo le diré a María que me compre el libro.* (I shall tell Maria to buy me the book.). *Dígale usted a Guillermo que escriba pronto.* (Tell William to write soon.). *Mis padres me prohiben que yo fume.* (My parents forbid

me to smoke.). *El insiste en que yo vaya con ella.* (He insists on my going with her.). *Los niños me piden que les compre regalos.* (The children are asking me to buy them presents.). *Yo prefiero que usted hable en español.* (I prefer that you speak Spanish.). *Esperamos que ustedes puedan venir esta noche.* (We hope you can come tonight.). *A mi madre no le gusta que yo salga.* (My mother does not like me to go out.). *Me alegro (de) que ustedes hayan venido.* (I am glad you have come.). *José me ha dicho que yo vaya esta noche.* (José has told me to go tonight.). *Yo siento que usted no venga conmigo,* (I am sorry you are not coming with me.). *Me sorprende que él haya dicho eso.* (I am surprised he said that.). *Yo temo que él no nos escriba.* (I am afraid he will not write to us.). *Yo dudo que ellos vengan.* (I doubt they will come.). *No creo que María esté en casa.* (I don't think Maria is at home.). *¿Cree usted que María esté en casa?* (Do you think Maria is at home?). Note that the indicative is used when the verb *dudar* (to doubt) is in the negative, and when the verb *creer* (to think, to believe) is in the affirmative: *Yo no dudo que ellos vendrán.* (I do not doubt they will come.). *Yo creo que María está en casa.* (I think Maria is at home.)

3. Use the subjunctive in impersonal expressions when the dependent verb has a subject (expressed or understood): *Es necesario que usted salga hoy.* (It is necessary for you to leave today.). *Es imposible que ella lo sepa.* (It is imposible for her to know that.). *Será conveniente que haga eso.* (It will be advisable for you to do that.). *Es increíble que ellos no hayan venido.* (It is incredible that they have not come.). *Será mejor que usted no lo compre.* (It will be better for you not to buy it.). *Es urgente que usted hable con él.* (It is urgent that you speak with him.). *Es preciso*

que usted esté aquí temprano. (It is necessary for you to be here early.). Note that the subjunctive is not used when the dependent verb has no subject, nor when the impersonal expressions denote certainty, even though the dependent verb has a subject: *Es imposible saber eso.* (It is impossible to know that.). *Es verdad que ella viene.* (It is true she is coming.)

THE IMPERFECT SUBJUNCTIVE

1. To use the imperfect subjunctive in the dependent clause, the verb in the main clause must be in the past (preterite), imperfect, or conditional indicative, and the verb must express volition (will), etc. (see The Present Subjunctive, 2, above). There is no difference between the *-ra* and the *-se* forms: *¿Quería usted que yo leyera* (or *leyese*)? (Did you want me to read?). *Ellos deseaban que usted saliera temprano.* (They wanted you to leave early.). *Yo temí que Elena no viniera.* (I was afraid Elena would not come.). *Yo le dije a María que me comprara el libro.* (I told Maria to buy me the book.). *Mis padres me prohibieron que yo fumara.* (My parents forbade me to smoke.). *Yo preferiría que ustedes vinieran más temprano.* (I should prefer that you come earlier.). *José me había dicho que yo fuera esta noche.* (José had told me to go tonight.). *El insistió en que yo fuera con ella.* (He insisted on my going with her.). *Fue necesario que usted saliera hoy.* (It was necessary for you to leave today.). *Era imposible que ella lo supiera.* (It was impossible for her to know that.)

2. When a verb of motion, feeling, belief, or doubt is in the present indicative, it may be followed by the imperfect subjunctive to express what you still feel about something that has already happened. Compare:

Yo siento que usted no venga conmigo—that you are not coming
Yo siento que usted no viniera conmigo—that you did not come

Yo no creo que ella venga—that she is coming
Yo no creo que ella viniera—that she came

Yo temo que ella vaya allá—that she will go there
Yo temo que ella fuera allá—that she went there

3. A statement or a polite request using *querer*, *poder*, or *deber* may be softened by using the *-ra* form of the imperfect subjunctive. Compare:

¿Quiere usted venir conmigo? Will you come with me?
¿Quisiera usted venir conmigo? Would you come with me?

Quiero mandar un cable a Washington. I want to send, etc.
Quisiera mandar un cable a Washington. I'd like to send, etc.

¿Puede usted decirme si voy bien para Madrid? Can you tell me, etc.
¿Pudiera usted decirme si voy bien para Madrid? Could you tell me, etc.

Usted no debe hacer eso. You mustn't do that.
Usted no debiera hacer eso. You shouldn't do that.

4. Use the imperfect subjunctive with *como si* (as if, as though): *Usted me mira como si no me comprendiera.* (You look at me as if you didn't under-

stand me.). *El habló como si fuera español.* (He spoke as if he were a Spaniard.)

Three further rules, governing the general use of the subjunctive mode, will be useful to the reader.

1. Use the subjunctive in the dependent clause when the antecedent is an indefinite or unknown person or thing expressed either by a noun or a pronoun: *Busco un hombre que hable español.* (I am looking for a man (any man) who speaks Spanish.). *Busco a alguien que hable español.* (I am looking for someone who speaks Spanish.). *No conozco a nadie que sepa hablar español.* (I don't know anybody who can (knows how to) speak Spanish.). *Necesito un hombre que sepa leer y escribir el español.* (I need a man who can (knows how to) read and write Spanish.). *No había nadie que pudiera decirme dónde estaba la tienda.* (There was nobody who could tell me where the store was.). *Quiero una camisa que sea buena y barata.* (I want a shirt which is good and yet cheap.) Note that the indicative is used when the antecedent is a definite or a known person or thing: *Busco al hombre que habla español aquí.* (I am looking for the man who speaks Spanish here.). *Conozco a alguien que habla español.* (I know someone who speaks Spanish.)

2. Use the subjunctive in the dependent clause after the conjunctions *a fin de que* (so that), *a menos que* (unless), *antes (de) que* (before), *con tal que* (provided that), *de manera que* or *de modo que* (so that), *para que* (so that), and *sin que* (without): *Iré a menos que llueva.* (I shall go unless it rains.). *Salí antes que él llegara.* (I left before he arrived.). *Yo se lo daré con tal que él me lo pida.* (I shall give it to him provided he asks me for it.). *Hábleme usted*

despacio a fin de que yo le entienda a usted. (Speak to me slowly so that I can understand you.). *Le hablé despacio a fin de que (para que, de modo que, de manera que) me comprendiera.* (I spoke to him slowly so that he could understand me.)

3. Use the subjunctive in the dependent clause with the following conjunctions to express future action: *así que, en cuanto, luego que,* or *tan pronto como* (as soon as); *aunque* (although); *cuando* (when); *después (de) que* (after); *hasta que* (until); *mientras que* (while); and *siempre que* (provided, whenever): *Yo se lo daré a ella tan pronto como (así que, en cuanto que, luego que) llegue.* (I shall give it to her as soon as she gets here.). *Dígale usted que se vaya cuando quiera.* (Tell her to go when she wants.). *Venga usted a verme después que ellos se vayan.* (Come and see me after they go away.). *Yo no saldré de casa hasta que termine el trabajo.* (I shall not leave the house until I finish the work.). *Los compraré siempre que me los dé usted baratos.* (I shall buy them provided you give them to me cheaply.) Note that the indicative is used when the action has taken place or is a customary, habitual fact: *Cuando estuve en Madrid paré en el Ritz.* (When I was in Madrid I stayed at the Ritz.). *Cuando voy a Madrid paro en el Ritz.* (When (whenever) I go to Madrid I stay at the Ritz.)

Conditional Sentences

Sentences having an "if" clause and a "result" clause are called conditional sentences. There are three classes of conditional sentences:

1. In a condition which is capable of fulfillment, the verbs are in the indicative; the "result" clause

may, however, use a verb in the imperative. This is true in English, except that Spanish *si* is not as a rule followed by the future or conditional indicative, nor by the present subjunctive: *Si tengo dinero, compraré el sombrero,* or *Compraré el sombrero si tengo dinero.* (If I have the money, I shall buy the hat—or, I shall buy the hat if I have the money.). *Si Elena viene, le daré los billetes.* (If Elena comes, I shall give her the tickets.). *Si ando mucho, me canso.* (If I walk too much, I get tired.). *Si José viene, dígale que pase.* (If José comes, tell him to come in.). *Si José vino anoche, trajo la carta.* (If José came last night, he brought the letter.)

Note: Don't use the future or conditional indicative or the present subjunctive after *si.* However, when *si* means "whether (if)," these tenses may be used after *si* if *si* is preceded by a clause which contains the verb *no saber: No sé si Elena vendrá esta noche.* (I don't know whether (if) Elena will come tonight.). *Yo no sé si podré ir a Europa.* (I don't know whether I shall be able to go to Europe.). *No sé si ella vendría anoche.* (I don't know whether Elena came last night.). *Yo no sé si pueda ir allá.* (I don't know whether I shall be able to go there.) *Si* may also be followed by the future or conditional in order to translate "I wonder whether (if)": *Si estarán aquí y yo no lo sé.* (I wonder whether they are here and I don't know it.). *Si estarían aquí.* (I wonder whether they were here.)

2. In a condition which may or may not be capable of fulfillment, the verb in the *si* clause is in the imperfect subjunctive, *-ra* or *-se* form, and the verb in the "result" clause is in the conditional: *Si lloviera, me quedaría en casa.* (If it should rain (which it may or may not) I would stay home.)

3. In a condition which is incapable of fulfillment (a contrary-to-fact condition), the verb in the *si* clause is in the imperfect subjunctive, *-ra* or *-se* form (simple or compound), and the verb in the "result" clause is in the conditional (simple or compound): *Si tuviera dinero iría a Sud América.* (If I had the money, I would go to South America.) [Meaning: *No tengo dinero; pero si lo tuviera, iría a Sud América.* (I don't have the money; but if I had it, I would go to South America.)] *Si hubiera tenido dinero, habría ido a Sud América.* (If I had had the money, I would have gone to South America.) [Meaning: *Yo no tenía dinero; pero si lo hubiera tenido, habría ido a Sud América.* (I didn't have the money; but if I had had it, I would have gone to South America.)] *Si no hubiera tenido dinero, no habría ido a Sud América.* (If I hadn't had the money, I would not have gone to South America.) [Meaning: *Tenía dinero; pero si no lo hubiera tenido, no habría ido a Sud América.* (I had the money; but if I hadn't had it, I would not have gone to South America.)]

Vocabulary

ABBREVIATIONS

adj. = adjective
adv. = adverb
art. = article
conj. = conjunction
def. = definite
demonstr. = demonstrative
fem. = feminine
indef. = indefinite
inf. = infinitive
interj. = interjection
interr. = interrogative
masc. = masculine
neg. = negative
neut. = neuter
num. = number
obj. = object
op. = opposite of
part. = participle
pers. = person, personal
pl. = plural
poss. = possessive
p.p. = past participle
prep. = preposition
pres. = present tense
pret. = preterite tense
pron. = pronoun
reflex. = reflexive
rel. = relative
sing. = singular
vb. = verb

The number in parenthesis after each infinitive refers you to the model verb which has the corresponding number in Verb Charts.

a—*prep.* *(see p. 264)* to, at, in, into, on, etc.
abajo—*adv.* down, below; downstairs (*op.* arriba)
abierto—*p.p.* abrir, open; opened (*op.* cerrado)
abogado (el)—lawyer
abrazar (7)—to embrace
abrigarse (6)—to cover one's self; to put on a coat
abrigo (el)—overcoat; wrap
abril (el)—April
abrir (3)—to open; *p.p.* abierto (*op.* cerrar); se abre, it opens
abuelo (el)—grandfather; abuela (la), grandmother; *pl.*

grandparents

acá—*adv.* here, over here (*mostly motion, see p. 262*)

acabar (1)—to finish, to end; **acabar de** + *inf.* (*in the present and imperfect only*), to have just + *p.p.;* **acabar de** + *inf.* (*in any other tense*), to finish; **se acabó,** it is (was) over

acaso—*adv.* perhaps; **por si acaso,** just in case

aceite (el)—(olive) oil

aceptar (1)—to accept

acera (la)—sidewalk

acerca de—*prep.* concerning, about

acercarse (a) (5)—to come (go) near, to approach

acompañar (a) (1)—to come (go) with, to accompany

acordarse (de + *obj.*) (19)—to remember, to recollect (*op.* **olvidar, olvidarse de** + *obj.*)

acostarse (19)—to go to bed

acostumbrado—*p.p.* accustomed; **estar acostumbrado a,** to be accustomed (used) to

acostumbrar (1)—to accustom; **acostumbrarse (a),** to get used to

acuerdo (el)—agreement; **estar de acuerdo (con),** to agree (with)

adelantar (1)—to advance; to gain time, to be fast; **se adelanta,** it (*a timepiece*) is fast *op.* **atrasar**)

¡adelante!—come in!

además *adv. & conj.* besides, moreover; **además de,** *prep.* besides

¡adiós!—goodbye

adonde *see* **donde**

¿adónde? *see* **¿dónde?**

adorno (el)—ornament, decoration

afeitarse (1)—to shave

afortunadamente—*adv.* fortunately (*op.* **desafortunadamente**)

agosto (el)—August

agradable—*adj.* pleasant (*op.* **desagradable**)

agradar (1)—to please

agradecer (12)—to be thankful for

agua (el, *but fem.*)—water

aguardar (1)—to wait, to wait for

¡ah!—oh! (*expressing surprise*)

ahí—*adv.* there; **ahí está,** there it is

ahora—*adv.* now; **ahora mismo,** right now; **ahora bien,** now then

aire (el)—air

al (a + el)—to the (*see p. 244*); **al** + *inf.,* on (when, upon) + *pres. part.*

alcoba (la)—bedroom

alegrarse (de) (1)—to be glad (to *or* of)

alegre—*adj.* gay, cheerful (*op.* **triste**)

algo—*indef. pron.* something (*op.* **nada**); **algo de (nuevo),** something (new); *adv.* somewhat, a little

algodón (el)—cotton

alguien—*indef. pron.* someone, somebody (*op.* **nadie**)

algún—*used instead of* **alguno** *before a masc. sing. noun*

alguno—*indef. pron.* someone, anyone, some, any; *indef. adj.*

some, any; **algunos,** some, a few

alimentar (1)—to feed; **alimento** (el), food

alma (el, *but fem.*)—soul

almorzar (19, 7)—to have (eat) lunch

almuerzo (el)—lunch, luncheon

alquilar (1)—to rent; **alquiler** (el), rent, rental

alrededor—*adv.* around, about; **alrededor de,** *prep.* around

alto—*adj.* high; tall; **en voz alta,** in a loud voice, aloud

alumno (el)—pupil; **alumna** (la), pupil

allá—*adv.* there, over there (*mostly motion, see p. 262*)

allí—*adv.* there, over there

amable—*adj.* kind, pleasant

amar (1)—to love

ambos—*indef. adj. & pron.* both

amigo (el)—friend; **amiga** (la), friend; **querida amiga,** my dear (friend)

amor (el)—love; **es un amor,** she (he, it) is a darling

ancho—*adj.* wide, broad; loose (*of clothing*)

andar (25)—to walk, to go (*without definite destination*); to run (*of machines*)

anoche—*adv.* last night

ante—*prep.* before (*in position or order*); in the presence of

antes—*adv.* before (*in time*), sooner (*op.* **después**); **antes de,** *prep.* before; **antes (de) que,** *conj.* before

antiguo—*adj.* old, ancient (*of things*) (*op.* **nuevo**)

año (el)—year: **¿cuántos años tiene usted?** how old are you? **tengo trienta y dos años,** I am thirty-two years old; **cumpleaños** (el), birthday

apagar (6)—to put out, to turn off (*a fire, a light*) (*op.* **encender**)

apellido (el)—(family) name

apenas—*adv.* hardly, scarcely

apreciar (1)—to appreciate

aprender (a) (2)—to learn (to) (*by study or effort*)

aquel, aquella—*demonstr. adj.* that, that . . . over there; **aquellos, aquellas,** those, those . . . over there

aquél, aquélla — *demonstr. pron.* that one, that one over there; **aquéllos, aquéllas,** those, those over there

aquello—*neut. pron.* that

aquí—*adv.* here; **aquí tiene usted (la llave),** here is (the key); **por aquí,** this way; around here

árbol (el)—tree

arreglar (1)—to arrange, to put in order; to repair

arriba—*adv.* up, above; upstairs (*op.* **abajo**)

asegurar (1)—to assure; to insure

así—*adv.* thus, so, like this (that), in this (that) way; **así es,** that's right

asiento (el)—seat

asistir (a) (3)—to attend, to be present

asunto (el)—matter, affair, business; subject

atrasar (1)—to delay; to be slow (*a timepiece*); **el reloj se atrasa,** the watch is slow

atreverse (a) (2)—to dare; **no**

me atrevo a hablar, I don't dare to speak
aun (=**hasta**)—*adv.* even, still; **aun cuando,** even though, even
aún (=**todavía**)—*adv.* yet, still; **aún no,** not yet; **más aún,** still more, furthermore
aunque—*conj.* although, even though
autobús (el)—bus
automóvil (el) — automobile, car (*also* **el auto, el coche**)
avenida (la)—avenue
averiguar (8)—to find out, to make sure, to verify
avión (el)—plane, airplane
avisar (1)—to inform, to send (leave) word, to let (someone) know
ayer—*adv.* yesterday
ayuda (la)—help, aid
ayudar (a) (1)—to help (to)
azúcar (el)—sugar
azul—*adj.* blue

B

bailar (1)—to dance
bajar (1)—to go (come) down; to get off (*op.* **subir**)
bajo—*adj.* short; low; soft (*of sound*) (*op.* **alto**); *prep.* under, below
banco (el)—bank
bañarse (1)—to bathe
barato—*adj.* cheap (*op.* **caro**)
bastante—*adv.* enough; rather, fairly; *indef. adj. & pron.* enough, plenty of
bastar (1)—to be enough
beber (2)—to drink
besar (1)—to kiss
biblioteca (la)—library
bien—*adv.* well; clearly, perfectly; **¡bien!** fine! good! **está bien,** (that's) all right; **muy bien,** very well (*op.* **mal**)
biftec (el)—steak
billete (el)—ticket (*also* **el boleto**); bill, bank note
blanco—*adj.* white (*op.* **negro**)
blusa (la)—blouse
boca (la)—mouth
bolsa (la)—purse, stock exchange
bolsillo (el)—pocket
bondadoso—*adj.* kind, good-natured
bonito—*adj.* pretty, nice (*op.* **feo**)
botones (el)—bellboy, page
brazo (el)—arm
buen—*used instead of* **bueno** *before a masc. sing. noun* (*op.* **mal**)
bueno—*adj.* good; well (*in health*) (*op.* **malo**); **¡bueno!** good! fine!
buscar (5)—to look for, to seek; to call for; to get; **buscar un médico,** to get a doctor

C

caballero (el)—gentleman, sir
caber (26)—to be room for, to fit; **cabe (en la caja),** there is room for it (in the box); **no cabe duda,** there is no doubt
cabeza (la)—head
cabo (el)—end; cape (*in geography*); **al cabo de,** *prep.* at the end of; **llevar a cabo,** to carry out, to accomplish
cada—*indef. adj.* each, every;

cada uno (una), each one; **cada tres días,** every three days; **cada quince días,** every two weeks; **cada vez que (vengo),** every time (I come); **cada vez más** (+ *adj.*), more and more
caer (27)–to fall; to be situated; **caerse,** to fall; **se cayó,** he (she, it) fell
café (el)–coffee; café
caja (la)–box, case; **en la caja,** at the (cashier's) desk
cajón (el)–drawer
calcetín (el)–sock
calidad (la)–quality
caliente–*adj.* hot, warm (*applied only to things that can attain high temperatures, not to weather or persons*); **café caliente,** hot coffee; **agua caliente,** hot water (*op.* **frío**)
calor (el)–heat, warmth (*op.* **frío**); **hace calor,** it is warm (*of the weather*); **tengo calor,** I am warm (hot) (*of a person*)
callar (1)–to be silent, to keep still
calle (la)–street; **salió a la calle,** he went out
cama (la)–bed
camarero (el)–waiter
cambiar (1)–to change; to exchange
cambio (el)–change; exchange; **en cambio,** on the other hand
caminar (1)–to walk, to travel
camino (el)–road; way
camisa (la)–shirt
campo (el)–country (*as opposed to city*); field
cansar (1)–to tire out; **cansarse,** to get tired; **estar cansado,** to be tired
cantar (1)–to sing
capaz–*adj.* capable, able
capital (la)–capital (*of a country* or *state*)
cara (la)–face
cariño (el)–affection
carne (la)–meat; flesh
caro–*adj.* dear, expensive (*op.* **barato**)
carretera (la)–highway, road
carta (la)–letter
cartera (la)–pocketbook; wallet; brief case
casa (la)–house; business firm; **a (la) casa,** home; **en casa,** at home; **en casa de,** at the house of
casado–*adj.* married
casar (1)–to marry, to marry off; **casarse,** to get married; **casarse con,** to marry
casi–*adv.* almost, nearly
caso (el)–case, affair; **hacer caso de,** to pay attention to
casualidad (la)–chance, coincidence; **por casualidad,** by chance
catorce–fourteen
causa (la)–cause; **a causa de,** *prep.* because of
celebrar (1)–to celebrate; to be glad of
cena (la)–supper
cenar (1)–to have (eat) supper
centavo (el)–cent
cepillo (el)–brush
cerca–*adv.* near, near by (*op.* **lejos**); **cerca de,** *prep.* near, nearly
cero–zero
cerrar (17)–to close, to shut (*op.* **abrir**)

cielo (el)—sky; heaven

cien—*used instead of* **ciento** *before the word modified:* **cien hombres (mujeres)**, one hundred men (women)

ciento—*used before another number:* **ciento cinco**, one hundred and five

cierto—*adj.* certain, true; a certain; **es cierto**, it is certain; **por cierto**, certainly; come to think of it

cinco—five

cincuenta—fifty

cine (el)—movies

cita (la)—appointment, "date"

ciudad (la)—city

claro—*adj.* clear, bright; light (*in color*); **¡claro!** surely! of course!

clase (la)—class; sort, kind

cliente (el, la)—customer, client

clima (el)—climate

cobrar (1) to charge; to collect

cocina (la)—cooking; kitchen

coger (9)—to pick; to catch

colgar (6)—to hang, to hang up

colocar (5)—to place, to put

color (el)—color

comedor (el)—dining room

comenzar (17, 7)—to begin, to start

comer (2)—to eat; to dine

comida (la)—food; meal; dinner

como—*rel. adv. & conj.* as, like, such as; when; since; provided that; **como antes**, as before; **como de costumbre (ordinario)**, as usual; **tal como**, such as; **tan pronto como**, as soon as; **como si**, *conj.* as if

¿cómo? — how? why? what? **¿cómo es (la casa)?** what is (the house) like? **¿cómo no?** of course! certainly! **¡cómo no!** why certainly! **¿cómo se llama esto en español?** what do you call this in Spanish? **¿cómo se dice . . . en español?** how does one say . . . in Spanish?

cómodo—*adj.* comfortable

compañero (el), **compañera** (la)—companion

compra (la)—purchase; **ir de compras**, to go shopping

comprar (1)—to buy (*op.* **vender**)

comprender (2)—to understand

común—*adj.* common

con—*prep.* with; by, etc. (*op.* **sin**); **con cuidado**, carefully

conducir (13)—to drive; to conduct, to lead

conmigo—with me

conocer (12)—to know, to be acquainted with; to meet, to make the acquaintance of; to recognize; **conocerse**, to know each other

conseguir (23, 1)—to get, to obtain; to succeed in

consejo (el)—counsel, piece of advice

considerar (1)—to consider, to regard

consiguiente: por consiguiente, therefore, as a result, consequently

consistir en (3)—to consist of

contar (19)—to count; to tell (a story); **contar con**, to count on

contento—*adj.* pleased, satisfied
contestar (a) (1)—to answer
continente (el)—continent
continuar (14)—to continue, to go on
contra—*prep.* against
contrario—*adj.* contrary, opposite; **al contrario,** on the contrary; **lo contrario,** the opposite
convenir (44)—to be proper, to be suitable; to agree, to concur
conversación (la)—conversation
convidar (1)—to invite
copa (la)—stemmed glass, goblet
corazón (el)—heart; courage
corbata (la)—necktie
cordero (el)—lamb
correr (2)—to run; to hurry
cortar (1)—to cut, to cut off
cortés—*adj.* polite, courteous
corto—*adj.* short (*op.* **largo**)
cosa (la)—thing; matter, affair; **cosa así,** something of the sort; **otra cosa,** something else
costar (19)—to cost
costilla (la)—rib; chop; **costillas de cordero,** lamb chops
costumbre (la)—habit, custom; **como de costumbre,** as usual
creer (15)—to believe; to think; **creo que sí,** I think so; **creo que no,** I don't think so; **¡ya lo creo!** I should say so!
criado (el)—servant; **criada (la),** servant, maid
cruzar (7)—to cross
cuadra (la)—block (*of houses*)
cual—*rel. pron.* (such) as; **el cual; la cual, los cuales, las cuales,** who, which, that; **cual,** *adv.* as, like
¿cuál?—*adj. & pron.* which? which one? what?
cualquier *or* **cualquiera**—*indef. adj. & pron.* any, anyone, any . . . at all
cuando—*adv. & conj.* when; **cuando más,** at (the) most
¿cuándo?—when?
cuanto—*rel. adj. & pron.* as much as, as many as; all that; *rel. adv.* as much as, as far as; **en cuanto,** *conj.* as soon as; **en cuanto a,** *prep.* as for; **cuanto más . . . tanto más,** the more . . . the more; **unos cuantos,** a few
¿cuánto?—how much? **¿cuántos?** how many? **¿cuántos años tiene usted?** how old are you?
cuarenta—forty
cuarto—*adj.* fourth; **cuarto (el),** room; quarter
cuatro—four
cuchara (la)—spoon
cucharita (la)—teaspoon
cuchillo (el)—knife
cuello (el)—neck; collar
cuenta (la)—account; bill (*for goods or services*); **dar cuenta de,** to report on; **darse cuenta de,** to realize, to be aware of; **tener en cuenta,** to keep in mind, to take into consideration
cuerpo (el)—body
cuestión (la)—question (*for discussion*), problem; **ser cuestión de,** to be a question of
cuidado (el)—care, caution; **¡cuidado!** look out! be care-

ful! **tener cuidado,** to be careful

cuidar (1)—to take care (of), to be careful; **cuidarse,** to take care of oneself

culpa (la)—fault, blame, guilt; **echar la culpa a,** to blame; **tener la culpa de,** to be to blamed for

cuyo—*rel. poss. adj.* whose

Ch

chaleco (el)—vest

chaqueta (la)—jacket, coat

chico (el)—small boy, youngster; **chica (la),** little girl

chocolate (el)—chocolate

D

daño (el)—damage; harm

dar (28)—to give; to strike (*of clocks*); to take (a walk): **vamos a dar un paseo (una vuelta),** let's take a walk; **dar a,** to face, to open on, to overlook: **la ventana da al parque,** the window overlooks the park; **dar con,** to meet, to find: **di con María en la calle,** I met Mary in the street; **dar los buenos días (las buenas tardes, las buenas noches),** to say (wish) good morning (afternoon *or* evening, night); **darse la mano,** to shake hands; **darse prisa,** to hurry: **¡dese usted prisa!** hurry up!; **dar gracias,** to thank; **dar calor,** to be warm: **este vestido da mucho calor,** this dress is too warm; *see* **cuenta**

de—*prep.* of; from; than; about; in (*after superlative*); by; with, in (*see p. 252*); **el (la los, las) de** (*see p. 251*); **del que (de la que,** *etc.*)(*see p. 260*); **de algún modo,** in some way

debajo—*adv.* underneath, under (*op.* **encima**); **debajo de,** *prep.* under (*op.* **encima de, sobre, en**)

deber (2)—to owe; *as an auxiliary expressing obligation:* **deber** + *inf.*, ought, should, ought to have, should have, have to: **usted debe salir en seguida,** you ought to leave at once; *as an auxiliary expressing supposition, probability, or belief:* **deber de** + *inf.*, must, must have: **él debe de haber salido,** he must have gone out; **debe de ser verdad,** it must be true

deber (el)—duty

debido a—owing to, due to

debiera *see p. 313*

débil—*adj.* weak (*op.* **fuerte**)

decidir (3)—to decide to; **decidirse a,** to make up one's mind to

decir (29)—to say; to tell; **es decir,** that is (to say)

declarar (1)—to state, to declare

dedo (el)—finger; toe

dejar (1)—to leave: **dejé el libro en casa,** I left the (my) book at home; to allow, to let, to permit: **no me dejaron entrar,** they didn't let me in; **déjeme usted en paz,** let (leave) me alone; **dejar de,** to stop, to leave off: **dejé de estudiar hace mucho tiempo,** I stopped studying a long time ago; **no dejar de,** not to fail to, to be sure to: **no deje usted de escribir,** don't fail (be sure) to write; **dejar caer,** to drop, to let fall; **dejar dicho,** to leave word (orders)

del (de + el)—of (from) the (*see p. 244*)

delante—*adv.* in front, before (*op.* **detrás**); **delante de,** *prep.* in front of (*op.* **detrás de**)

delgado—*adj.* thin (*op.* **gordo**)

delicioso—*adj.* delightful; delicious

demás—*indef. adj. & pron.*: **el (la, los, las) demás,** the rest, the other (others); **lo demás** (*neuter*), the rest, what is left

demasiado—*adj.* too much; **demasiados,** too many; **demasiado (demasiados) . . . para,** too much (many) . . . to; *adv.* too, too much

dentro—*adv.* inside, within (*op.* **fuera**); **dentro de,** *prep.* within, inside of; **dentro de poco,** in a little (short) while

derecho—*adj.* right; straight; **a la derecha,** on (at, to) the right (*op.* **a la izquierda**); **la mano derecha,** the right hand; **derecho (el),** right, privilege; law; **tener derecho a,** to have a right to

desafortunadamente—*adv.* unfortunately (*op.* **afortunadamente**)

desayunarse (1)—to eat breakfast

desayuno (el)—breakfast

descansar (1)—to rest

descanso (el)—rest

desconocer (12)—to ignore, to fail to recognize

describir (3)—to describe

desde—*prep.* since (*of time*); from (*of place*); **¿desde dónde?** from where? **¿desde cuándo?** since when? how long? (*op.* **hasta**); **desde hace** (+ *a period of time*) = for (+ *a period of time*); **desde luego,** of course; **desde que,** *conj.* since (*of time*)

desear (1)—to wish, to desire

deseo (el)—wish, desire

desgracia (la)—misfortune; **por desgracia,** unfortunately

despacio—*adv.* slowly, slow; **vaya usted despacio,** go slow

despacho (el)—office

despedir (23)—to dismiss, to discharge; **despedirse de,** to say goodbye to, to take leave of; **despedida (la),** farewell

despertar (17)—to awaken; **despertarse,** to awake, to wake up

después—*adv.* after, later, afterward; then (*op.* **antes**); **después de,** *prep.* after (*op.* **antes de**); **después que,** *conj.* after (*op.* **antes que**)

detener (41)—to detain, to stop; **detenerse,** to stop, to halt, to pause

detrás—*adv.* behind, in back (*op.* **delante**); **detrás de,** *prep.* behind, in back of (*op.* **delante de**)

devolver (20)—to give back, to return (*p.p.* **devuelto**)

día (el)—day (*op.* **(la) noche**); **al día siguiente,** (on) the next day; **a los pocos días,** within a few days; **mediodía** (*or* **medío día**) (el), noon; **buenos días,** good morning, goodday; **(en) todo el día,** all day long, the whole day; **hoy día,** nowadays; **ocho días,** a week; **quince días,** two weeks; **todos los días,** every day; **un día de estos,** one of these days

diciembre (el)—December

diente (el)—tooth

diez—ten

diferente—*adj.* different

difícil—*adj.* difficult, hard (*op.* **fácil**)

dinero (el)—money

Dios (el)—God; **¡Dios mío!** good heavens! dear me! oh dear; **¡por Dios!** for heaven's sake!

dirección (la)—direction; address

directamente—*adv.* directly

dirigir (9)—to direct; manage; **dirigirse a** (*a place*), to make one's way to (toward), to go to (toward); **dirigirse a** (*a person*), to address, to speak to

dispensar (1)—to excuse, to pardon; **¡dispense usted!** *or* **¡usted dispense!** excuse me!

disponer (36)—to dispose, to arrange; **disponer de,** to have at one's disposal; **disponerse a** + *inf.*, to get ready to

dispuesto—*adj.* (*and p.p.* **disponer**): **estar dispuesto (a),** to be ready (to), to be inclined (to)

distancia (la)—distance

distinguir (10)—to distinguish

diversión (la)—diversion, pastime

divertir (21)—to amuse; **divertirse,** to have a good time, to amuse oneself

doce—twelve

doler (20)—to ache, to feel pain, to hurt; **me duele la garganta,** I have a sore throat; **¿le duele la cabeza?** have you a headache?

dolor (el)—pain, ache; sorrow, grief; **tengo dolor de cabeza,** I have a headache

domingo (el)—Sunday; **el domingo,** on Sunday

don—Don (*a title of courtesy used without the article before a man's first name; it has no English equivalent*)

donde—*rel. adv.* where, in which, to which (*place*); **a donde** (*or* **adonde**), where, to which (*place*); **de donde,** from where, from which (*place*)

¿dónde?—where? **¿a dónde?** (*or* **¿adónde?**)

doña—Doña (*a title of courtesy used without the article before a lady's first name; it has no English equivalent*)

dormir (22)—to sleep; **dormirse,** to fall asleep

dos—two; **los dos,** both

ducha (la)—shower (*bath*)

duda (la)—doubt; **no cabe duda,** there is no doubt; **sin duda,** doubtless, no doubt

dudar (1)—to doubt

dueño (el), **dueña** (la)—owner

dulce—*adj.* sweet; **dulce (el),** sweet, sweetmeat
durante—*prep.* during, for
durar (1)—to last
duro—*adj.* hard (*to the touch*); stern (*op.* **blando**)

E

e—*conj.* and (*used instead of* **y** *before words beginning with* **i** *or* **hi,** *but not with* **hie**): **padre e hijo,** father and son; *but:* **agua y hielo,** water and ice
echar (1)—to throw, to cast; to pour (liquids); **echar a perder,** to spoil, to ruin; **echar de menos,** to miss
edad (la)—age
edificio (el)—building
efecto (el)—effect; **en efecto,** as a matter of fact, that's right
ejemplo (el)—example; **por ejemplo,** for example, for instance
el—*def. art. masc.* the (*see p. 243*),; **el** *instead of* **la**: *directly before a fem. sing. noun beginning with stressed* **a** *or* **ha:** **el agua,** the water; *but:* **la buena agua,** the good water; **las aguas,** the waters; **el** *instead of poss. adjs., p. 250;* **el de,** the one, he, *p. 252;* **el que,** the one that, he who, *p. 253;* **el cual,** who, which, that, *p. 258*
él—*pers. pron.* he; him; it (*masc.*)
elegir (23, 9)—to choose, to select; to elect
ella—*pers. pron.* she; her; it (*fem.*)
ellas—*pers. pron.* they; them (*pl. of* **ella**)
ello—*neut. pron.* it
ellos—*pers. pron.* they; them (*pl. of* **él**)
embargo: sin embargo—*conj.* however, nevertheless, still
emparedado (el)—sandwich
empezar (a) (17, 7)—to begin (to); **empezar por (decir),** to begin by (saying)
emplear (1)—to employ; to use
empleo (el)—employment, job; use
en—*prep.* in; on; at
encantado—*adj.* delighted
encantador—*adj.* charming; delightful
encantar (1)—to charm; to love (to like): **me encantan las flores,** I love flowers
encargar (6)—to order, to request; **encargarse de,** to take charge of, to be in charge of
encender (18)—to light; to turn on (*the light*) (*op.* **apagar**)
encima—*adv.* on top, above (*op.* **debajo**); **encima de,** on top of, on, over (*op.* **debajo de**)
encontrar (19)—to find; to meet, to encounter; **encontrarse,** to find oneself; to be: **ella se encuentra enferma,** she is sick
enero (el)—January
enfermo—*adj.* ill, sick
ensalada (la)—salad
enseñar (1)—to teach; to show
entender (18)—to understand
enterarse (de) (1)—to find out (about)
entonces—*adv.* then
entrada (la)—entrance; ticket;

sacar una entrada, to get (buy) a ticket
entrar (en) (1)—to enter, to go in, come in (*op.* **salir**)
entre—*prep.* between; among; **entre tanto,** in the meantime, meanwhile
entregar (6)—to deliver, to hand over
entretanto—*adv.* meanwhile (*same as* **entre tanto**)
enviar (14)—to send
esa, ésa *see* **ese, ése**
escribir (3)—to write
escrito—*p.p.* **escribir,** written
escritorio (el)—desk
escuchar (1)—to listen, to listen to, to hear
escuela (la)—school
ese, esa, *demonstr. adj.* that; **esos, esas,** those
ése, ésa—*demonstr. pron.* that one, that; **ésos, ésas,** those
eso—*neut. pron.* that; **¡eso es!** that's right! that's it! **por eso (lo hice),** that's why (I did it)
espalda (la)—shoulder; back
español—*adj.* Spanish, **español (el),** Spanish (*the language*); Spaniard
espárrago (el)—asparagus
espejo (el)—mirror, looking glass
esperanza (la)—hope
esperar (1)—to hope; to wait, to wait for; to expect; **le espero aquí,** I am waiting for you here
esposa (la)—wife
esposo (el)—husband
esquina (la)—corner (*street or object, but seen from the outside*); **doblar la esquina,** to turn the corner
esta, ésta *see* **este, éste**
estación (la)—railroad station; season
estado (el)—state; condition
estar (30)—to be (*see p. 300*); **estar de acuerdo (con),** to agree (with); **estar de (en) pie,** to stand; **estar de vuelta,** to be back; **estar para** + *inf.*, to be about to: **estaba para telefonear a usted,** I was about to telephone you; **estar por** + *inf.*, to be in favor of; **estar seguro de que,** to be sure that; **¡ya está!** all finished; that's all there's to it!
este (el)—east; **al este de,** east of
este, esta—*demonstr. adj.* this; **estos, estas,** these
éste, ésta—*demonstr. pron.* this one, this; **éstos, éstas,** these
esto—*neut. pron.* this; **por esto,** for this reason; this is why
estrecho—*adj.* narrow; tight (*of clothes*) (*op.* **ancho**)
estrella (la)—star
estudiar (1)—to study
estudio (el)—study; studio
excelente—*adj.* excellent
explicar (5)—to explain
extrañarse de (1)—to be surprised at

F

fábrica (la)—factory
fácil—*adj.* easy (*op.* **difícil**)
falda (la)—skirt
falta (la)—fault; lack, want; **me hace falta (dinero),** I need (money); **sin falta,** without fail

faltar (1)—to lack, to need, to be . . . short: **me faltan cinco dólares,** I am five dollars short; **faltan diez minutos para las dos,** it is ten minutes of (short of) two
familia (la)—family
favor (el)—favor; **¡por favor!** please! **haga (hágame) el favor de** + *inf.*, please; **me hace el favor de** + *inf.*, please; **si me hace el favor,** if you please
febrero (el)—February
fecha (la)—date (*of the month*)
feliz—*adj.* happy
feo—*adj.* ugly, homely (*op.* **hermoso**)
fin (el)—end; object, purpose; (*op.* **el principio**); **a fin de,** *prep.* in order to; **al fin,** at last; **en fin,** in short; anyway; **por fin,** finally; **un sin fin de,** a lot of, an endless number of; **a fines de,** toward the end
fino—*adj.* fine; delicate; of good quality; polite, courteous
flor (la)—flower
formar (1)—to form
frase (la)—phrase; sentence
frente (el)—front; **frente** (la), forehead; **en frente de,** *prep.* in front of; **frente a,** facing, opposite
fresco (el)—cool; **hace fresco,** it is cool; **fresco,** *adj.* cool; fresh; **hace una noche fresca,** it is a cool evening (night); **carne fresca,** fresh meat
frío (el)—cold; **hace frío,** it is cold (*of the weather*); **tengo frío,** I am cold (*of a person*); **frío,** *adj.* cold (*op.* **caliente,** *see* **caliente**); **hace una noche fría,** it is a cold evening (night); **el café está frío,** the coffee is cold
frito—*adj.* fried
fruta (la)—fruit
fuera—*adv.* outside, out (*op.* **dentro**); **fuera de,** *prep.* outside of
fuerte—*adj.* strong (*op.* **débil**)
fuerza (la)—force, power, strength
fumar (1)—to smoke; **se prohibe fumar,** no smoking
futuro (el)—future; **futuro,** *adj.* future

G

gana (la)—appetite, desire; **tener gana (ganas) de (comer, beber,** *etc.*), to feel like, to have a desire to (eat, drink, *etc.*)
ganar (1)—to win; to gain; to earn
gasolina (la)—gasoline
gastar (1)—to spend (*money*); to waste
general—*adj.* general; **en general,** generally; **por regla general,** as a general rule
generalmente—*adv.* generally
género (el)—class, kind; gender; material, dry goods
gente (la)—people; **mucha gente,** many people; **dos (tres, cuatro,** *etc.*) **personas,** two (three, four, *etc.*) people; **el pueblo norteamericano,** the American people
gordo—*adj.* fat (*op.* **delgado**)

gorra (la)—cap
gozar (7)—to enjoy; **gozar de** + *obj.*, to enjoy
gracia (la)—grace, wit; **gracias,** thanks; **gracias a Dios,** thank Heaven; **gracias a,** *prep.* thanks to; **dar las gracias,** to thank
gran—*used instead of* **grande** *before a sing. noun,* great: **un gran hombre,** a great man; **una gran mujer,** a great woman
grande—*adj.* big, large; great (*op.* **pequeño**)
guante (el)—glove
guardar (1)—to keep, to store, to put away; to guard
guerra (la)—war
guisante (el)—pea
gustar (1)—to please, to like; **me gustan los libros,** I like (the) books; **¿le gusta el libro?** do you like the book?
gusto (el)—pleasure; taste; liking; **tanto gusto en conocerle,** *or* **mucho gusto en conocerle,** (so) glad to meet you, "how do you do"; **con mucho gusto,** with pleasure, gladly

H

haber (4)—(*used to form perfect tenses*) to have (*see p. 303*): **haber** + *p.p.*, to have + *p.p.*: **yo he (usted, él, ella ha, nosotros hemos, ustedes, ellos, ellas han) hablado (comido, vivido,** *etc.*), I have (you have, he, she has, we have, you, they have) spoken eaten, lived, *etc.*); **haber de** + *inf.*, to be to: **él ha de salir mañana,** he is to leave tomorrow; **haber,** there is, there are (*impersonal 3rd pers. sing. only; pres. tense,* **hay**): **hay, había, hubo, habrá,** *etc.*, there is, are, there was, were, there will be, *etc.*: **¿había muchas personas en la fiesta?** were there many people at the party? **haber que** + *inf.*, to be necessary, must: **hay que ir en seguida,** it is necessary to (one must) go at once
habichuela (la)—bean
habitación (la)—room
hablar (1)—to speak; **hablar en voz alta,** to speak loudly; **hablar con,** to speak to; **oír hablar de,** to hear of, to hear about
hacer (32)—to make, to do; to have (*someone*) do (*something*); **hacer buen (mal) tiempo,** to be good (bad) weather; **hacer calor (frío),** to be warm (cold) (*weather*); **hacer caso de,** to pay attention to; **hacer falta,** to lack, to need; **hacer una pregunta,** to ask a question; **hacer un viaje,** to take a trip; **hacer el favor** (*see* **favor**); **hace una hora** (*or another expression of time*), an hour ago, *if main verb is in the pret.* (*see p. 304*), *but* for an hour, *if main verb is in the pres.* (*see p. 304*); **hacerse daño,** to hurt oneself
hacia—*prep.* toward
hallar (1)—to find (*op.* **perder**);

hallarse, to be found; to be: **me hallo muy cansado,** I am very tired
hambre (el, *but fem.*)—hunger; **tener hambre,** to be hungry
hasta—*prep.* as far as, up to, to; until, till; **hasta ahora,** so far, thus far; **hasta luego,** until later, see you later; **hasta que,** *conj.* until; **hasta,** *adv.* even, still
hay; hay que — *impersonal forms of* **haber** (*see* **haber**)
hecho—*p.p.* **hacer,** made, done; **hecho** (**el**), fact, deed, act
helado (**el**)—ice cream
hermano (**el**)—brother; **hermana** (**la**), sister
hermoso—*adj.* beautiful, handsome; fine
hijo (**el**)—son; **hija** (**la**), daughter; **los hijos,** children
historia (**la**)—history; story
hombre (**el**)—man; **¡hombre!** well! say! what! look here! man alive!
hora (**la**)—hour; time (*of day*); **¿a qué hora?** when? at what time? **a las tres,** at three o'clock; **¿qué hora es?** what time is it? **ser hora de,** to be time to: **es hora de salir** (**comer,** *etc.*), it is time to leave (to eat, *etc.*)
hotel (**el**)—hotel
hoy—*adv.* today; **hoy mismo,** this very day; **hoy día,** nowadays
huevo (**el**)—egg; **huevos fritos** (**revueltos, pasados por agua**) fried (scrambled, soft-boiled) eggs
huir (16)—to flee, to run away
humaho—*adj.* human
humedad (**la**)—humidity, dampness

I

ida (**la**)—going; **un billete de ida y vuelta,** a round-trip ticket
idea (**la**)—idea
idioma (**el**)—language
iglesia (**la**)—church
igual—*adj.* equal; the same; *pl.* alike
impermeable (**el**)—raincoat
importante—*adj.* important
importar (1)—to import; to matter, to mind, to be important; **no importa,** never mind; **¿qué importa?** what difference does it make?
imposible—*adj.* impossible (*op.* **posible**)
indicar (5)—to indicate, to show
insistir (3)—to insist; **insistir en,** to insist on
instante (**el**)—instant, moment
inteligente—*adj.* intelligent
intención (**la**)—intention; **tener intención de,** to intend to
interesante—*adj.* interesting
inútil—*adj.* useless (*op.* **útil**)
invierno (**el**)—winter
invitar (1)—to invite
ir (33)—to go (*op.* **venir**); **irse,** to go away, to leave: **¿se va usted?** are you leaving? **ir a** + *inf.*, to be going to: **voy a telefonear a mi mujer,** I am going to telephone my wife; **ir a buscar,** to go for: **voy a buscar mi sombrero,** I am going for my hat; **ir bien**

para (*a destination*), to go in the right direction for (*a destination*); **ir de compras**, to go shopping; **ir por** (*same as* **ir a buscar**), to go for; **vamos**, we are going; let's go; let's; **¡vamos!** come on! come now!; **¡vamos a ver!** let's see!
izquierdo—*adj.* left (*op.* **derecho**; **a la izquierda**, at (to, on the left; **la mano izquierda**, the left hand

J

jabón (el)—soap
jamás—*adv.* never, not . . . ever (*see p. 263*)
jamón (el)—ham
jardín (el)—flower garden
joven—*adj.* young (*op.* **viejo**); **joven (el, la)**, young man, young woman
juego (el)—game
jueves (el)—Thursday
jugar (19, 6)—to play, to frolic; **jugar a**, to play (*a game*)
jugo (el)—juice
julio (el)—July
junio (el)—June
junto—*adj.* joined; **juntos**, together; **junto a**, *prep.* next to, close to, beside

K

kilómetro (el)—kilometer

L

la—*def. art. fem.* the (*see p. 243*); **la** *instead of possessive adjectives, p. 250;* **la de**, the one, she, *p. 252;* **la que**, the one that, she who, *p. 253;* **la cual**, who, which, that, *p. 258;* **la**, *pers. pron.* her, you, it (*see p. 253*)
labio (el)—lip
lado (el)—side; **al lado de**, *prep.* next to, beside, at the side of; **al otro lado de la calle**, across the street
lámpara (la)—lamp
lana (la)—wool
lápiz (el)—pencil
largo—*adj.* long (*op.* **corto**)
las—*def. art. fem. pl.* the (*see p. 243*); **las** *instead of poss. adjs., p. 250;* **las de**, the ones, those, *p. 252;* **las que**, those who, who, which, the ones that, *p. 253;* **las cuales**, who, which, that; **las**, *pers. pron.* them; you, *p. 253*
lástima (la)—pity; **¡qué lástima!** what a pity!
lavar (1)—to wash; **lavarse**, to wash oneself
le *pers. pron.* (*see p. 253*) him, you; to (for, from) him, to (for, from) you, to (for, from) her
lección (la)—lesson
leche (la)—milk
lechuga (la)—lettuce
leer (15)—to read
legumbre (la)—vegetable
lejos—*adv.* far, far off, far away (*op.* **cerca**); **a lo lejos**, in the distance; **lejos de**, *prep.* far from
lengua (la)—language; tongue
les *pers. pron.* (*see p. 253*) them you; to (for, from) them; to

for, from) you
letra (la) (*of the alphabet*) letter
levantar (1)—to raise, to lift; **levantarse,** to get up, to rise
libre—*adj.* free; vacant; off
libro (el)—book
ligero—*adj.* light (*in weight*); swift; *adv.* fast, swiftly
limpiar (1)—to clean; to wipe off
limpio—*adj.* clean (*op.* **sucio**)
lista (la)—list; **lista de platos,** menu
listo —*adj.:* **estar listo,** to be ready; **ser listo,** to be clever
lo—*def art. neut.* (*see p. 255*) *used before adjs., p.p.s, and advs.:* **lo malo,** the bad (thing), that which is bad; **lo pasado,** the past, that which is past; **a lo lejos,** in the distance; *with the superlative of advs.* (*see p. 262*)*:* **vine lo más pronto posible,** I came as soon as possible; **lo** + *adj. or adv.* + **que** + *vb.*, how + *adj. or adv.* + *vb.:* **¡lo bien que habla!** how well he speaks!; **lo de,** that, that business of, that affair of; **lo que,** *rel. pron.* that which, what, *p. 258;* **lo,** *pers. pron.* him; you; it, *p. 253*
lodo (el)—mud, mire
lograr (1)—to obtain, to win, to accomplish; **lograr** + *inf.*, to succeed in + *pres. part.:* **logré hablar con ella,** I succeeded in talking to her
los *def. art. masc. pl.* the (*see p. 243*)*;* **los** *instead of poss. adjs., p. 250;* **los de,** the ones, those, *p. 252;* **los que,** those who, who, which, the ones that, *p. 253;* **los cuales,** who, which, that; **los,** *pers. pron.* them, you, *p. 253*
luces (las)—lights
luego—*adv. & conj.* then, next; soon; **desde luego,** of course; right away; **hasta luego,** see you later, until later; **luego que,** as soon as
lugar (el)—place, spot; **en lugar de,** instead of, in place of
luna (la)—moon
lunes (el)—Monday
luz (la)—light

Ll

llamar (1)—to call; **llamar (a la puerta),** to knock (at the door); **llamar la atención (a alguien),** to attract (someone's) attention; **llamar por teléfono,** to call up (on the telephone); **llamarse,** to be called, to be named: **se llama María,** her name is María; **¿cómo se llama usted?** what is your name?
llave (la)—key
llegada (la)—arrival
llegar (6)—to arrive, to reach, to get: **llegué por la mañana,** I arrived in the morning; **llegar a** (+ *inf. or place*), to come to, to reach: **llegó a creerlo,** he came to believe it; **llegaremos a la ciudad,** we shall reach the city; **llegar a ser,** to become, to come to be
llenar (1)—to fill

lleno—*adj.* full (*op.* **vacío**); **lleno de,** full of

llevar (1)—to take, to carry; to wear; **llevarse,** to take away, to carry off; **llevarse con,** to get along with (someone)

llorar (1)—to cry, to weep

llover (20)—to rain; **está lloviendo,** it is raining

lluvia (la)—rain

M

madera (la)—wood

madre (la)—mother

maestro (el), **maestra** (la)—teacher

mal—*used instead of* **malo** *before a masc. sing. noun;* **mal,** *adv.* badly, poorly; **mal** (el), evil; illness

maleta (la)—suitcase

malo—*adj.* bad; wicked; ill; **estar malo,** to be ill; **ser malo,** to be bad, to be wicked

mandar (1)—to order, to command; to send; **mandar hacer,** to order (have) made; **mandar por,** to send for

manera (la)—way, manner; **de esta manera,** in this way; **de manera que,** *conj.* so that, in such a way that

mano (la)—hand

mantequilla (la)—butter

manzana (la)—apple

mañana (la)—morning; **(a las diez) de la mañana,** (at ten o'clock) in the morning; **por la mañana,** in the morning; **mañana,** *adv.* tomorrow; **mañana por la mañana,** tomorrow morning

mapa (el)—map

mar (el, la)—sea; **el Mar Cantábrico,** Cantabrian Sea

maravilloso—*adj.* marvelous

marchar (1)—to march; to walk, to go; **marcharse,** to go away, to leave

marido (el)—husband

martes (el)—Tuesday

marzo (el)—March

más—*indef. adj., pron.,* and *adv.* more; most; rather (*see p. 260*); **cada vez más,** more and more; **más allá,** farther on; **más de,** more than; **más o menos,** more or less; **no . . . más que,** only

matar (1)—to kill

mayo (el)—May

mayor—*adj.* greater, greatest; larger, largest; elder, older, oldest, *p. 262*; **la mayor parte** (*or* **la mayoría**) **de,** most of, the majority, the greater part of

me—*pers. pron.* me, to (for, from) me; myself, *p. 253*

media (la) — stocking (*see* **medio**)

medianoche (la) (*or* **media noche**), midnight

medicina (la)—medicine

médico (el)—doctor, physician

medio—*adj.* half, a half; **la una y media,** half past one; **media hora,** a half-hour, half an hour; *adv.* half; **medio** (el), middle; means; **en medio de,** *prep.* in the middle of; in the midst of; **por medio de,** by means of

mediodía (el) (*or* **medio día**), noon

mejor—*adj. & adv.* better; best (*see p. 262*); **el (la) mejor,** the best; **lo mejor,** the best thing; **mejor dicho,** rather
memoria (la) — memory; **de memoria,** by heart
menor—*adj.* lesser; smaller; younger; youngest; **el (la) menor,** the youngest
menos—*indef. adj. & pron., and adv.* less; least; **a menos que,** unless; **al menos** (*or* **a lo menos, por lo menos**), at least; **cada vez menos,** less and less; **echar de menos,** to miss; **lo menos posible,** as little as possible; **no poder menos de,** not to be able to help
menudo: a menudo—often, frequently (*op.* **rara vez**)
mes (el)—month
mesa (la)—table
meter (2)—to put in, to put inside, insert (*op. sacar*); **meterse en** (*a place*), enter; **meterse con,** to pick a quarrel with
mi—my (*see p. 249*)
mí—me (*see p. 256*)
miedo (el)—fear; **tener miedo,** to be afraid
mientras—*conj.* while; **mientras que,** while (*in contrast*); **mientras tanto,** meanwhile
miércoles (el)—Wednesday
mil (el)—thousand
millón (el)—million; **un millón de (dólares),** a (one) million (dollars)
minuto (el)—minute
mío—mine (*see p. 250*)
mirar (1)—to look, to look at
mismo—*adj.* same; very; self; **el mismo libro,** the same book; **la misma mañana,** the same morning; **ahora mismo,** this very moment, right now; **hoy mismo,** this very day; **yo mismo,** I myself; **ellos mismos,** they themselves
mitad (la)—half; middle
modo (el) — way, manner; means; **de este (ese) modo,** in this (that) way; **de ningún modo,** by no means, not at all, at all; **de algún modo,** in some way; **de tal modo,** so, in such a way; **de todos modos,** anyway, anyhow, at any rate; **de modo que,** *conj.* so that; and so
molestar (1)—to bother, to disturb; to irritate; **molestarse,** to trouble oneself
momento (el)—moment, minute
montaña (la)—mountain
moreno—*adj.* brunette, dark (*op.* **rubio**)
morir (22)—to die (*op.* **nacer**)
motivo (el)—ground, reason, cause; **con motivo de,** because of
mover (20)—to move (*to change place or position*)
mozo (el)—boy, young fellow; servant; porter; waiter
muchacho (el)—boy; **muchacha (la),** girl; **los muchachos,** the children; the boys
mucho—*indef. adj. & pron., and adv.* much, a lot of; long (*of time*); very; greatly, hard, a good deal, a lot; **no tengo mucho tiempo,** I haven't

much time; **tengo mucha sed,** I am very thirsty; **él estudia mucho,** he studies a great deal; **muchas veces,** many times, often
muerte (la)—death
muerto—*p.p.* **morir,** dead; died; **él ha muerto,** he has died; **él está muerto,** he is dead
mujer (la)—woman; wife
mundo (el)—world; people; **todo el mundo,** everybody
música (la)—music
muy—*adv.* very (*not used before* **mucho;** *don't say* **muy mucho,** *but* **mucho** *or* **muchísimo**)

N

nacer (12)—to be born
nada—*indef. pron. & adv.* nothing, not . . . anything (*op.* **algo**), not at all; **nada de nuevo,** nothing new; **nada más,** nothing else, nothing more, no more; **nada que hacer** (**leer,** *etc.*), nothing to do (to read, *etc.*); **no me extraña nada,** it doesn't surprise me at all
nadie—*indef. pron.* nobody, no one, not . . . anybody (*op.* **alguien**)
naranja (la)—orange; **jugo de naranja,** orange juice
nariz (la)—nose
natural—*adj.* natural; native
navaja (la)—pen knife; razor
necesario—*adj.* necessary; **me es necesario** (**hablar**), it is necessary for me (to speak)
necesitar (1)—to need, to be in need of
negar (17, 6)—to deny; to refuse; **negarse a,** to refuse to
negocio (el)—deal, affair, business; **negocios,** business
negro—*adj.* black (*op.* **blanco**)
nevar (17)—to snow; **está nevando** (*or* **nieva**), it is snowing
ni—*adv. & conj.* nor, not . . . or; **ni . . . ni,** neither . . . nor; and not; not even; **ni mucho menos,** far from it; **ni siquiera** (**cinco centavos**), not even (five cents); **ni yo tampoco,** nor I either, neither do (am) I
niebla (la) fog
nieto (el)—grandson; **nieta** (la) granddaughter; **nietos** (los), grandchildren
nieve (la)—snow
ningún—*used instead of* **ninguno** *before a masc. sing. noun* (*op.* **algún**)
ninguno—*indef. adj. & pron.* no, not . . . any, no one, none, nobody, not . . . anybody; **de ningún modo,** not at all, by no means, at all; **en ninguna parte,** nowhere
niña (la)—child, girl, little girl
niño (el)—child, boy, little boy
no—*adv.* no, not; **¿no? ¿no es verdad?** isn't that so? isn't it true?
noche (la) night (*op.* **día**); **de noche,** by (at) night; **esta noche,** tonight; **media noche** (*or* **medianoche**), midnight; **por la noche,** in the evening, at night; **todas las noches,** every night; **buenas noches,**

good evening, good night
nombre (el)—name; noun
norte (el)—north; **al norte de,** north of
nos—*pers. pron.* us, to (for, from) us, ourselves, *see p. 253*
nosotros—*pers. pron.* we; us; ourselves
noticia (la)—notice, piece of news; **noticias,** news; **tener noticias de,** to hear from, to have news of
novecientos—nine hundred
noventa—ninety
noviembre (el)—November
nublado—*adj.* cloudy
nuestro—our, ours (*see p. 249*)
nueve—nine
nuevo—*adj.* new; **de nuevo,** again; **algo de nuevo,** something new
número (el)—number (*see p. 40*); **número de teléfono,** telephone number
nunca—*adv.* never, not . . . ever

O

o—*conj.* or
objeto (el)—object, article; purpose
obra (la)—work, book
octubre (el)—October
ocupado—*adj.* busy
ocupar (1)—to occupy; **ocuparse de,** to busy oneself with, to take care of, to attend to
ochenta—eighty
ocho—eight; **ocho días,** a week
oeste (el)—west; **al oeste de,** west of
oficina (la)—office
ofrecer (12)—to offer; **¿qué se le ofrece?** what can I do for you? what would you like?
oído (el)—hearing; (inner) ear
oír (34)—to hear; **oír decir,** to hear said; **oír hablar de,** to hear of, to hear about
ojalá (que)—would (that), I hope (that), I wish (that); **¡ojalá!** I hope so!
ojo (el)—eye
oler (20)—to smell; **oler a,** to smell of
olor (el)—smell, odor
olvidar (1)—to forget; **olvidarse de,** to forget; **olvidársele,** to forget: **se me olvidó traer el libro** (*or* **olvidé traer el libro,** *or* **me olvidé de traer el libro),** I forgot to bring the book
once—eleven
opinión (la)—opinion
oponerse a (36)—to oppose, to be opposed (to) to be against, to object to (that)
oportunidad (la)—opportunity
orden (el)—order, relation; **orden (la),** order, command; **a sus órdenes,** at your service, I am glad to be of service
oreja (la)—(outer) ear
oro (el)—gold
otoño (el)—autumn, fall
otro—*indef. adj. & pron.* other, another, another one; **otra cosa,** another thing, something else, anything else; **otra vez,** again; **el uno al otro,** each other; **los otros,** the others

P

padre (el)—father; **padres (los),**

parents, father and mother
pagar (6)—to pay, to pay for, to pay back
página (la)—page
país (el)—country, nation
pájaro (el)—bird
palabra (la)—word
pan (el)—bread; **pan con mantequilla,** bread and butter; **pan tostado,** toast
pantalón (el), **pantalones** (los)—trousers, pants
pañuelo (el)—handkerchief
papel (el)—paper; rôle, part
paquete (el)—package
par (el)—pair; couple (*of things*)
para—*prep.* for, to, in order to (*see p. 267*); **para que,** *conj.* in order that, that; **¿para qué?** for what purpose? what's the use? why?
parada (la)—stop, halt
paraguas (el)—umbrella
parar (1)—to stop; **pararse,** to stop; to stand up
parecer (12)—to seem, to appear; **parece,** it seems; **parecen,** they seem; **me (le, nos, les) parece,** it seems to me (to you, to him, to her, *etc.*) I (*etc.*) guess; **parece mentira,** it's hard to believe; **si le (les) parece,** if it's all right with you; **¿qué le (les) parece?** how do you like it? how does it strike you? what do you think of it? **parecerse a,** to resemble, to look like: **me parezco a mi padre,** I look like my father
parecer (el)—opinion; **a mi parecer,** in my opinion; **al parecer,** apparently; **cambiar de parecer,** to change one's mind
pariente (el)—relative
parque (el)—park
parrilla (la)—grill; **a la parrilla,** grilled
parte (la)—part; **de parte de,** in the name of; **en ninguna parte,** nowhere; **en todas partes,** everywhere; **la mayor parte de,** most of; **tomar parte en,** to take part in
pasado (el)—past; *adj.* past, last; **el año pasado,** last year; **la semana pasada,** last week
pasajero (el)—passenger
pasar (1)—to pass; to pass by; to come in; to spend (*time*); to happen, to take place; **pasar por,** to pass by; **¿qué pasa?** what's going on? what's the matter? **¿qué le pasa (a usted)?** what's wrong with you? what's the matter with you? **¡que usted lo pase bien!** good luck (to you)!
pasear (1)—to take a walk, to take a ride; **pasear en automóvil,** to take a ride
paseo (el)—walk; ride; drive, boulevard; **ir de paseo,** to go for a walk
paso (el)—step, pace; **dar un paso,** to take a step
pasta (la)—paste
patata (la) *or* **papa** (la)—potato
pecho (el)—chest
pedazo (el)—piece
pedir (23)—to ask, to ask for; to order (*a meal*); **¿se los**

pidió usted? did you ask him for them?; **pedir prestado**, to borrow
pegar (6)—to stick, to paste; to fasten, to set; to hit, to beat, to strike; to sew
peinarse (1)—to comb (one's hair)
peine (el)—comb
película (la)—film
peligro (el)—danger
pelo (el)—hair
pena (la)—grief, sorrow, trouble; **vale la pena**, it is worth while; **no vale la pena**, it isn't worth while
pensar (17)—to think; **pensar** + *inf.*, to intend to; **pensar en** + *inf. or obj.*: **pensé en ir allá**, I thought of going there; **pensé en usted**, I thought of you; **pensar de**, to think about, to have an opinion of: **¿qué piensa usted de ese hombre (este libro**, *etc.*)? what do you think of that man (of this book, *etc.*)?; **eso ni pensarlo**, that's out of the question; **sin pensar**, without thinking, carelessly, thoughtlessly
peor—*adj. & adv.* worse, worst (*comparative of* **malo**, *p. 261*)
pequeño—*adj.* small, little (*op.* **grande**)
pera (la)—pear
perder (18)—to lose; to waste (*time*); to miss (*a train*); **perder de vista**, to lose sight of; **echar a perder**, to spoil, to ruin; **perderse**, to get lost, to lose one's way
pérdida (la)—loss
perdón (el)—forgiveness; pardon
perdonar (1)—to forgive; to pardon; to excuse; **¡perdóneme! ¡perdone usted!** excuse me!
periódico (el)—newspaper
permitir (3)—to allow, to permit; **me permite usted**, allow me, please
pero—*conj.* but (*see p. 263*)
persona (la)—person; **personas**, persons, people
pesar (1)—to weigh; **pesar** (el), grief, trouble; **a pesar de**, *prep.* in spite of
pescado (el)—fish (*as food, or out of the water*); **pez** (el), fish (*alive, or in the water*)
peseta (la)—peseta (*Spanish monetary unit*)
peso (el)—weight; peso (*monetary unit of some Spanish-American countries*)
pie (el)—foot; **a pie**, on foot; **de pie**, standing; **en pie**, standing, on foot; **ponerse en pie**, to stand up
pierna (la)—leg (**pata** (la), *of a table, chair, etc.*)
piso (el)—floor, story; apartment
placer (el)—pleasure
planta (la)—plant, bush
plata (la)—silver
plato (el)—plate; dish
playa (la)—beach
plaza (la)—square (*in a city*)
pluma (la)—pen; feather
pobre—*adj.* poor (*op.* **rico**); **el (la) pobre**, the poor man (woman)
poco—*indef. adj. & pron.* little, (a) few; short (*of time*); **a**

poco, presently; **poco a poco,** little by little, gradually; **por poco (por un poco, a poco más, de poco),** almost; **un poco de (agua,** *etc.*), a little (water, *etc.*); **a los pocos días,** within a few days; **unos pocos,** a few; **poco,** *adv.* little

poder (35)—to be able, can, could; to be possible, may, might; **no poder menos de,** not to be able to help; **poder (el),** power

polvo (el)—dust; powder; **hay polvo,** it is dusty

pollo (el)—chicken; **pollo asado,** roast chicken

poner (36)—to put, to place, to set; **ponerse,** to put on (*clothing*); **ponerse (bien, enfermo),** to become (well, sick); **ponerse a (trabajar),** to start (working); **ponerse en marcha,** to set out, to start off; **ponerse en (de) pie,** to stand up

por—*prep.* by, for; along; in, through (*see p. 267*); **por aquí,** this way; around here; **por bueno (grande, caro,** *etc.*) **que sea,** however good large, expensive, *etc.*) it may be; **por eso,** for that reason, that's why; **por favor,** please; **por la mañana,** in the morning; **por lo visto,** apparently; **por poco,** almost; **por si acaso,** in case; **por supuesto,** of course; **¿por qué?** why?

porque—*conj.* because; for

posible—*adj.* possible (*op.* **imposible**); **hacer lo posible por,** to do one's best for; **lo más pronto posible,** as soon as possible

postre (el)—dessert

precio (el)—price

preciso—*adj.* precise, exact; **ser preciso,** to be necessary

preferir (21)—to prefer

pregunta (la)—question; **contestar a la pregunta,** to answer the question; **hacer una pregunta,** to ask a question

preguntar (1)—to ask (*a question*); **preguntar por,** to inquire about, to ask for

preparar (1)—to prepare, to get ready

presentar (1)—to present, to introduce (*socially*); **presentarse,** to introduce oneself; to appear

presente—*adj.* present; **presente (el),** the present (*time*)

presidente (el)—president

prestar (1)—to lend, to loan; **prestar atención,** to pay attention

primavera (la)—spring (*the season*)

primer—*used instead of* **primero** *before a masc. sing. noun,* first

primero—*adj.* first, former (*op.* **último**); *adv. & conj.* first

principal—*adj.* principal, main

prisa (la)—hurry, haste; **de prisa,** fast, hurriedly; **darse prisa,** to hurry; **tener prisa,** to be in a hurry

probar (19)—to prove; to test, to try out; to taste, to sample; **probarse,** to try on (*an article of clothing*)

profesor (el), **profesora** (la)—professor, teacher

prohibir (3)—to prohibit, to forbid; **se prohibe** + *inf.*, **no** + *pres. part.*: **se prohibe fumar,** no smoking

prometer (2)—to promise (to)

pronto—*adv.* soon; **de pronto,** suddenly; **lo más pronto posible,** as soon as possible; **tan pronto como,** as soon as

pronunciar (1)—to pronounce; to utter

propina (la)—tip, gratuity

propósito (el)—purpose, intention; **a propósito,** by the way; **de propósito,** on purpose

próximo—*adj.* next; nearest

proyecto (el)—plan, project

público (el)—public; audience

pudiera (*see p. 313*)

pueblo (el)—town; people: **el pueblo español,** the Spanish people

puerta (la)—door; **llamar a la puerta,** to knock (at the door)

pues—*adv.* well, so; then; **pues bien,** well then, very well; **pues,** *conj.* for, because, since

puesto—*p.p.* **poner,** put, placed; **puesto que,** since, inasmuch as; **puesto** (el), job, position; place; stand, booth

punto (el)—point; **a punto de,** *prep.* on the point of; **al punto,** immediately; **en punto,** on the dot, exactly (*of time*)

puro—*adj.* pure

Q

que—*rel. pron.* who, whom, which, that (*see p. 257*); when (*referring to a noun of time*); **el (la, los, las) que,** who, the one (those) who (which, that); **que,** *conj.* that; for, because; than (*after a comparative*); **creo que sí,** I think so; **creo que no,** I don't think so

¿qué?—*adj. & pron.* what? **¿para qué?** what for? **¿por qué?** why? **¿qué tal?** hello, how are you? **¡qué!** what! what a! (*followed by a noun*): **¡qué vida!** what a life! **¡qué mujer más hermosa!** what a beautiful woman!; **¡qué!** how! (*followed by an adj. or adv.*): **¡qué hermosa es!** how beautiful she is! **¡qué raro!** how odd! **¡qué bien habla!** how well he speaks!

quedar (1)—to remain, to be (have) left: **quedan dos billetes,** there are two tickets left; **me queda un dólar,** I have one dollar left; **quedar grande (pequeño,** *etc.*), to be too large (small, *etc.*): **estos zapatos me (le, nos, les) quedan grandes,** these shoes are too big for me (for you, for him, *etc.*); **quedarse,** to remain, to stay: **¿se queda usted?** are you staying?

quejarse (1)—to complain; **quejarse, de,** to complain about

querer (37)—to wish, to want; to be willing, will (*see p. 304*); **no quiero éstos,** I don't want these; **¿quiere usted venir conmigo?** will you come with me?; **querer,** *in the past, also means* to refuse *and* to try: **no quiso**

contestarme, he refused to answer me; **quisimos comprarlos, pero no quedaban más**, we tried to buy them, but there were no more left; **querer decir**, to mean: **¿qué quiere decir esa palabra?** what does that word mean?; **querer a**, to love, care for (*a person*): **quiero a mis hijos**, I love my children; **quisiera** (*imperfect subjunctive*), I should like, you (he, *etc.*) would like, *see p. 313*
querido—*adj.* dear, beloved; **querido amigo**, (my) dear friend
queso (el)—cheese
quien—*rel. pron. used only of person* (*pl.* **quienes**), who, whom; he (she, *etc.*) who; anyone who, *see p. 258*
¿quién? (*pl.* **¿quiénes?**)—*pron.* who? whom? **¿de quién?** whose?
quince—fifteen
quinientos—five hundred
quinto—*adj.* fifth
quisiera (*see p. 313*)
quitar (1)—to take away, to take off, to remove; **quitarse** + *an article of clothing*, to take off, to remove
quizás, quizá—perhaps, maybe

R

radio (la) —radio; **radio** (el), radio (set); **tengo un radio**, I have a radio; **escucho la radio**, I listen to the radio
rápido—*adj.* rapid, swift, fast; **rápido** (el), express (*train*)
raro—*adj.* rare; odd, strange, curious; **¡qué raro!** how odd!; **rara vez**, rarely
rato (el)—(a) while, (a) short time
razón (la)—reason; **tener razón**, to be right; **no tener razón**, to be wrong
recado (el)—message; errand
recibir (3)—to receive
recién—*adv. used before p.p.s*, recently, newly, just: **recién casado** (**llegado**, *etc.*), newly wed (arrived, *etc.*)
reciente—*adj.* recent
recoger (9)—to pick up, to pick; to gather, to collect
recomendar (17)—to recommend
recordar (19)—to remember, to recall; to remind
recuerdo (el)—souvenir, remembrance; recollection; **recuerdos** (los), regards, greetings, best wishes
regalar (1)—to give (*a present*)
regalo (el)—present, gift
reír, reírse (24)—to laugh; **reírse de**, to laugh at
reloj (el)—clock, watch
repente: de repente—suddenly, all of a sudden
repetir (23)—to repeat
resolver (20)—to decide; solve (*a problem*); **resolverse**, to make up one's mind; **resolverse a**, to decide to, to determine to
respecto a—*prep.* in regard to
respeto (el)—respect
respirar (1)—to breathe
responder (2)—to reply, to answer; to respond
respuesta (la)—reply, answer
restaurante (el)—restaurant

resuelto—*p.p.* **resolver,** decided; solved
resultado (el)—result
resultar (1)—to result, to turn out (to be), to prove (to be)
revista (la)—magazine; review
rico—*adj.* rich, wealthy (*op.* **pobre**); delicious (*of food*)
rincón (el)—corner (*room or object, but seen from the inside*)
río (el)—river
rojo—*adj.* red
romper (2)—to break; to tear, to tear open
ropa (la)—clothing, clothes; **ropa blanca,** household linen; **ropa interior,** underwear
roto—*p.p.* **romper,** broken
rubio—*adj.* blond (*op.* **moreno**)
ruido (el)—noise

S

sábado (el)—Saturday
saber (38)—to know, to know how, can: **no sé dónde está,** I don't know where he is; **¿sabe usted tocar el piano?** can you (do you know how to) play the piano?; to find out: **no lo supe hasta ayer,** I didn't find out until yesterday; **saber a,** to taste of: **esto sabe a agua,** this tastes of (like) water; **saber de,** to have heard from, to know of: **ayer supe de mi familia,** I heard from my family yesterday; **no sé nada de eso,** I don't know anything about that
sacar (5)—to draw (out), to take out, to get out (*op.* **meter**)
saco (el)—sack coat, jacket; bag, sack
sal (la)—salt
sala (la)—living room; room
salida (la)—way out, exit; departure, leaving
salir (39)—to go out, to come out, to get out, to leave; **salir de casa,** to go out; **salir a la calle,** to go out (into the street); **salir de compras,** to go out shopping; **salir a comprar,** to go out to buy; **salir para,** to leave for
salud (la)—health
saludar (1)—to say hello to, to greet, to bow to
saludo (el)—greeting, bow
San—(*contraction of* **Santo**) Saint (*used before masculine proper nouns*); **San Sebastián,** San Sebastian (*seaport and summer resort in the north of Spain*)
sangre (la)—blood
se (*see p. 255*)—*pers. pron. used instead of* **le** *and* **les** (to you, to him, to her, to them) *before* **la, lo, los,** *and* **las; se,** *reflex, pron.* (*see p. 253*) yourself, himself, *etc.*; **se,** *reciprocal pron.* each other, to each other, one another; **se,** *used instead of passive* (*see p. 257*)
secar (5)—to dry; **secarse,** to dry
seco—*adj.* dry
secretaria (la)—secretary
sed (la)—thirst; **tener sed,** to be thirsty

seda (la)—silk
seguida (la)—succession; **en seguida,** at once, right away
seguir (23, 10)—to follow; to keep on, to go on, to continue
según—*prep.* according to; *conj.* according to what
seguramente—*adv.* surely, certainly
segundo (el)—second; *adj.* second
seguro—*adj.* sure, certain; safe, secure; **de seguro,** surely; **estar seguro de,** to be sure of; **estar seguro de que,** to be sure that
seis—six
sello (el)—stamp
semana (la)—week; **la semana que viene,** next week; **la semana pasada,** last week; **(el) fin de semana,** (the) week end
semejante—*adj.* similar, like, alike; such a; **semejante precio (hombre, mujer,** *etc.*), such a price (man, woman, *etc.*)
sentar (17)—to seat; **sentarse,** to sit down
sentido (el)—sense; meaning; **sin sentido,** unconscious; meaningless
sentir (21)—to be sorry, to regret; **sentir que,** to be sorry that; **lo siento,** I am sorry (about it); to hear (*a vague sound*): **siento ruido,** I hear (a) noise; **sentirse** + *adj. or adv.,* to feel + *adj. or adv.:* **me siento bien,** I feel well; **¿cómo se siente usted?** how do you feel?
señal (la)—sign, signal
señalar (1)—to point out, to point (to); to mark
señor (el)—gentleman; lord; sir (*in direct address*); Mr. (*as a title*)
señora (la)—lady; wife; madam (*in direct address*); Mrs. (*as a title*)
señorita (la)—young lady; Miss (*in direct address and as a title*)
septiembre (el)—September
séptimo—*adj.* seventh
ser (40)—to be (*see p. 298*); *auxiliary of the passive voice, see p. 300;* **a no ser que,** unless; **ser de,** to belong to; to be made of; **ser hora de,** to be time for (to); **es decir,** that is to say; **es que,** the fact is that, it's because; **es la una,** it's one o'clock; **son las dos,** it's two o'clock; **¿qué ha sido de (ella)?** what has become of (her); **soy yo,** it is I; **son los niños,** it is the children
serio—*adj.* serious; reliable; **en serio,** seriously
servilleta (la)—napkin
servir (23)—to serve; to serve the purpose, to do; **servir de,** to serve as; **servir para,** to be good for; **esto no sirve para nada,** this is no good, this is good for nothing; **servirse,** to help oneself; **sírvase usted,** please help yourself; **servirse de,** to make use of
sesenta—sixty

setecientos—seven hundred
setenta—seventy
sexto—*adj.* sixth
si—*conj.* if; whether; **si bien,** although; **por si acaso,** in case; **si no,** otherwise, else; **si . . .,** why . . . (*often not translated, or translated by other expressions*): **si yo no lo quiero,** indeed (why), I don't want it; **si será verdad,** I wonder if it's true
sí—*adv.* yes; *often translated by an auxiliary*: **el no habla español, pero yo sí,** he does not speak Spanish, but I do; **nosotros no vamos, pero ellos sí,** we are not going, but they are; **sí que** + *clause,* certainly + *clause*
sí—*reflex. pron. obj. of prep., third person sing. and pl.* yourself, himself, herself, itself, themselves: **dijo para sí,** he said to himself
siempre—*adv.* always, ever (*op.* **nunca**); **siempre que,** provided that, whenever
siete—seven
significar (5)—to mean, to signify
siguiente—*adj.* following, next; **al dia siguiente,** (on) the next (following) day; **a la mañana siguiente,** the next morning
silla (la)—chair
simpático—*adj.* charming, appealing, congenial
sin—*prep.* without; **sin embargo,** nevertheless, however; **sin duda,** doubtless, without any doubt; **sin falta,** without fail; **sin que,** *conj.* without
sino—*conj.* (*see p. 263*) *used only after negatives,* but; **sino que,** but
siquiera—*adv.* at least, even; **ni siquiera,** not even
sitio (el)—place, spot, site
sobre—*adv.* on, upon; over, above; about, concerning; **sobre todo,** above all, especially; **sobre** (el), envelope
sobretodo (el)—overcoat
sobrino (el)—nephew; **sobrina** (la), niece
sol (el)—sun; **hace sol,** it is sunny; **hay sol,** the sun is shining
solamente—*adv.* only
soler (20)—*used only in the present and imperfect tenses followed by an infinitive,* to be in the habit of, to be wont to: **él suele decir eso,** he is wont to say that; *the imperfect is translated by* used to: **yo solía ir allá,** I used to go there
solo—*adj.* alone, only, single
sólo—*adv.* only; merely; **no sólo yo, sino usted,** not only I, but you
soltero (el)—bachelor, unmarried man; **soltera** (la), spinster, unmarried woman
sombrero (el)—hat
sonar (19)—to sound, to ring
soñar (19)—to dream; **soñar con,** to dream about
sopa (la)—soup
sorprender (2)—to surprise; **sorprenderse (de),** to be surprised (about)
su—your, his, her, its, their (*see p. 250*)

subir (3)—to go up, to come up; to bring up, to take up; to climb; to get in (*op.* **bajar**)
suceder (2)—to happen, to occur
sucio—*adj.* dirty (*op.* **limpio**)
sud—*used instead of* **sur** *before words beginning with a vowel:* **Sud América,** South America; **sudamericano (el),** (a) South American
suelo (el)—ground; floor
sueño (el)—sleep; dream; **tener sueño,** to be sleepy
suerte (la)—luck; **tener suerte,** to be lucky; **de suerte que,** *conj.* so that
suéter (el)—sweater
sufrir (3)—to suffer; to endure, to bear
suponer (36)—to. suppose, to assume
supuesto—*p.p.* **suponer,** supposed; **por supuesto,** of course
sur (el)—south; **al sur de,** south of
suyo—yours, his, hers, theirs (*see p. 251*)

T

tal—*indef. adj.* such, such a; **con tal que,** *conj.* provided that; **¿qué tal?** hello! how are you? **tal como,** just as, such as, as; **tal vez,** maybe, perhaps
también—*conj.* also, too (*op.* **tampoco**)
tampoco—*conj.* neither, not . . . either, nor . . . either; **ni yo tampoco,** nor I either, nor do I . . . either (*op.* **también**)
tan—*adv. used before adjs. and advs.,* so, as, such a; **él habla tan bien el español,** he speaks Spanish so well; **el sombrero es tan lindo,** the hat is so pretty; **tan . . . como,** as . . . as, (not) so . . . as; **él no habla tan bien como ella,** he does not speak so well as she
tanto (tantos)—*indef. adj. and pron.* as much, so much (as many, so many); **tanto . . . como (tantos . . . como),** as much . . . as, so much . . . as (as many . . . as, so many . . . as); **yo no tengo tanta hambre como usted,** I am not so hungry as you; **él tiene tanto tiempo como yo,** he has as much time as I; **ellos tienen tantos hijos como nosotros,** they have as many children as we; **tanto como (tantos como)** as much as, so much as (as many as, so many as); **no tengo tanto como usted,** I haven't so much as you; **entre tanto** (*same as* **entretanto**) or, **mientras tanto,** meanwhile; **por lo tanto,** therefore
tardar (1)—to delay, to be late; to take (*of time*); **tardar en,** to be slow in, to take time to; **¿cuánto tiempo tarda usted en ir a casa?** how long does it take you to get home? **tardé cinco minutos en llegar aquí,** it took me five minutes to get here
tarde—*adv.* late (*op.* **temprano**); **tarde (la),** after-

noon; **por la tarde,** in the afternoon; **el sábado por la tarde,** Saturday afternoon; **a las dos de la tarde,** at two o'clock in the afternoon; **buenas tardes,** good afternoon; **se hace tarde,** it is getting late; **se me hace (hizo, hará) tarde,** I am (was, will be) late

taza (la)—cup; **una taza de café,** a cup of coffee

teatro (el)—theater

telefonear (1)—to telephone

teléfono (el) — telephone; **llamar por teléfono,** to telephone; **número de teléfono,** telephone number

televisión (la)—television

temer (2)—to fear, to be afraid

temprano—*adv.* early (*op.* tarde)

tenedor (el)—fork

tener (41)—to have; to hold; **aquí tiene usted el libro,** here is the book; **tener buena cara,** to look well (healthy); **tener . . . años,** to be . . . years old; **tener cuidado,** to be careful; **no tener cuidado,** not to worry; **tener en cuenta,** to bear (keep) in mind, to take into account (consideration); **tener derecho a,** to have a right to; **tener fama de,** to have the reputation of, to be reputed to be; **tener (mucho) frío (calor),** to be (very) cold (warm); **tener ganas de** (+ *inf.*) to feel like; **tener (mucho) guesto en,** to be (very) glad to; **tener (mucha) hambre,** to be (very) hungry; **tener inconveniente en,** to object to; **tener intención de,** to intend to; **tener interés en,** to be eager to; **tener miedo (de),** to be afraid (of), to fear; **tener ocasión de,** to have an opportunity to; **tener paciencia,** to be patient; **tener . . . pies de alto (ancho, largo,** *etc.*), to be . . . feet tall (wide, long, *etc.*); **tener que** (+ *inf.*), to have to; **tener mucho (poco, nada) que** (+ *inf.*), to have a great deal (little, nothing) to; **tener que ver con,** to have to do with; **tener razón,** to be right; **no tener razón,** to be wrong; **tener sed,** to be thirsty; **tener sueño,** to be sleepy; **tener tiempo de,** to have time to; **¿cuántos años tiene usted?** how old are you? **¿qué tiene usted?** what is the matter with you?, what is wrong with you? **¿qué tiene usted en la mano?** what is the matter with your hand?, what have you in your hand? **aquí tiene usted,** here is (*used when demonstrating, pointing out, or handing over*)

tercero—*adj.* third

terminar (1)—to end, to finish; **terminar de** (+ *inf.*), to finish; **terminarse,** to finish, to be finished, to be over

tiempo (el)—time; weather; **a tiempo,** in time; **al mismo tiempo,** at the same time; **¿cuánto tiempo?** how long?

hace mal (buen) tiempo, the weather is bad (good); **mucho tiempo,** a long while; **no tengo tiempo,** I have no time; **poco tiempo,** a short while
tienda (la)—store, shop
tierra (la)—earth, land
tío (el)—uncle; old fellow; **tía (la),** aunt
tirar (1)—to throw, to throw away; to shoot; to pull; **tirar de,** to pull (on)
toalla (la)—towel
tocar (5)—to touch; to play (*a musical instrument*); **me toca a mí,** it is my turn; **le toca a usted,** it is your turn
tocino (el)—bacon
todavía—*adv.* yet, still; **todavía no,** not yet
todo—*indef. adj. & pron.* all, whole, entire, each, every; everything; **ante todo,** first of all; **sobre todo,** especially; **todo el día,** all day, the whole day; **toda la noche,** the whole night; **todo el mundo,** everybody; **todo lo posible,** everything possible; **todo lo que pude,** all (as much as) I could; **de todos modos,** at any rate, anyway; **por (en) todas partes,** everywhere; **todas las noches,** every night; **todos los días,** every day; todos, everyone, everybody
tomar (1)—to take; to drink, to have (*a beverage*); to have (*food*); to buy (*a ticket*); **tomar en serio,** to take seriously; **tomar parte en,** to take part in
tomate (el)—tomato
toronja (la)—grapefruit
tostado—*adj.* toasted; **pan tostado,** toast
trabajar (1)—to work
trabajo (el)—work
traer (42)—to bring
traje (el)—suit; dress
tratar (1)—to treat: **¿cómo los trataron?** how were you treated?, how did they treat you? **tratar de** (+ *obj.*), to deal with, to be about: **este libro trata de la historia de España,** this book is about (deals with) the history of Spain; **tratar de** (+ *inf.*), to try to: **traté de hacer lo que usted me dijo,** I tried to do what you told me; **tratarse de** (+ *obj. or inf.*), to be a question of, to be about: **se trata de hacerlo hoy mismo,** it is a question of doing it this very day; **no se trata de eso,** it isn't about that
través: a través de—*prep.* across
trece—thirteen
treinta—thirty
tren (el)—train
tres—three
triste—*adj.* sad

U

u—*conj.* or (*used instead of* **o** *before words beginning with* **o** or **ho**): **uno u otro,** one or another; **mujeres u hombres,** women or men
último—*adj.* last (*in a series*), latest (*op.* **primero**); **por último,** finally

un, una—*indef. art.* a, an; **unos, unas,** some; a pair of: **unos cinco pesos,** about five pesos; **unos zapatos,** a pair of shoes; **un** *is used instead of* **uno** *before a masc. sing. noun*
único—*adj.* sole, only
uno—one; *indef. pron.* one, someone; **unos,** some
uña (la)—nail (*of finger or toe*)
usar (1)—to use
usted—*pers. pron.* you; **ustedes,** *pl.*
útil—*adj.* useful

V

vacación (la)—vacation; *used mostly in the pl.:* **vacaciones**
valer (43)—to be worth; to cost; **¿cuánto valen los zapatos?** how much are these shoes? **(no) valer la pena,** (not) to be worth while; **(no) valer la pena de** (+ *inf.*), (not) to be worth while (*doing what the inf. expresses*)
vapor (el)—steam; steamship
varios—*adj. pl.* several
vaso (el)—glass (*for drinking*)
veces—*see* **vez**
vecino (el), vecina (la)—neighbor
veinte—twenty
vencer (11)—to overcome, to conquer, to defeat
vender (2)—to sell (*op.* **comprar**)
venir (44)—to come (*op.* **ir**); **venir (ir) a buscar,** to come (go) to look for, to come (go) to get; **el año que viene,** next year
ventana (la)—window
ver (45)—to see; **a ver,** *or* **vamos a ver,** let's see
verano (el)—summer
veras: de veras—really, truly
verdad (la)—truth; **es verdad,** it (that) is true; **la verdad es,** to tell the truth, the truth is; **¿no es verdad? ¿verdad?** isn't that so? isn't it true?
verdadero—*adj.* true, real
verde—*adj.* green
vergüenza (la)—shame
vestido (el)—dress
vestir (23)—to dress; **vestirse,** to dress, to put on clothes
vez (la)—time (*in a series*); **a la vez,** at the same time; **a veces,** at times; **alguna vez,** sometime, *in a question it means* ever: **¿ha estado usted alguna vez en México?** have you ever been in Mexico? **algunas veces,** sometimes; **cada vez más** (+ *adj.*), more and more; **cada vez que,** *conj.* every time that, whenever; **de una vez,** once and for all; **de vez en cuando,** from time to time; **dos veces,** twice; **en vez de,** *prep.* instead of; **muchas veces,** many times, often; **otra vez,** again, once more; **otras veces,** (some) other times; **por primera vez,** for the first time; **rara vez,** rarely, seldom; **tal vez,** maybe, perhaps; **una vez,** once
viajar (1)—to travel

viaje (el)—trip, journey; **buen viaje,** have a pleasant trip; **hacer un viaje,** to take a trip; **viaje de negocios,** business trip; **viaje de recreo,** a pleasure trip; **viaje por tren,** train trip
vida (la)—life (*op.* **muerte** (la)); **en mi vida,** never in my life
viejo—*adj.* old (*op.* **joven**)
viene—*from* **venir; el mes que viene,** next month; **la semana que viene,** next week; **el año que viene,** next year
viento (el)—wind; **hace viento,** it is windy
viernes (el)—Friday
vino (el)—wine; **vino blanco,** white wine; **vino tinto,** red wine
visitar (1)—to visit, to make a call
vista (la)—view; sight; **en vista de,** in view of; **perder de vista,** to lose sight of
visto—*p.p.* **ver,** seen; **por lo visto,** apparently
vivir (3)—to live
volar (19)—to fly
volver (20)—to come back, to go back, to return; to turn (*around*); **volver a** (+ *inf.*), to do again (*what the inf. expresses*): **volvió a telefonear esta tarde,** he telephoned again this afternoon
voz (la)—voice; **en voz alta,** in a loud voice, out loud, aloud; **en voz baja,** in a low voice, in an undertone; **dar voces,** to shout
vuelo (el)—flight
vuelta (la)—return; turn; **dar una vuelta,** to take a (short) walk; **estar de vuelta,** to be back; **un billete de ida y vuelta,** a roundtrip ticket
vuelto—*p.p.* **volver,** returned

Y

y—*conj.* and (*see* **e**)
ya—*adv.* already; by now; now; **¡ya lo creo!** I should say so! **ya está,** that's all there is to it; finished; **ya no,** no longer; **ya que,** *conj.* as long as, since; now that; **ya que no,** since (you are) not, although not
yo—*pers. pron.* I; **yo en su lugar,** if I were (*or* had been) you (he, she, they)

Z

zapato (el)—shoe